IF I STARTED TO CRY, I WOULDN'T STOP

What I talk about when I talked about football and Australia

IF I STARTED TO CRY, I WOULDN'T STOP

What I talk about when I talked about football and Australia

MATTHEW HALL

FAIRPLAY
PUBLISHING

First published in 2019 by Fair Play Publishing

PO Box 4101, Balgowlah Heights NSW 2093 Australia

www.fairplaypublishing.com.au

sales@fairplaypublishing.com.au

ISBN: 978-0-6484073-8-6

ISBN: 978-0-6484073-9-3 (ePUB)

© 2019 Matthew Hall

The moral rights of the author have been asserted.

All rights reserved. Except as permitted under the *Australian Copyright Act 1968* (for example, a fair dealing for the purposes of study, research, criticism or review), no part of this book may be reproduced, stored in a retrieval system, communicated or transmitted in any form or by any means without prior written permission from the Publisher.

Design and typesetting by Retta Laraway, Looksee Design.

Front cover photograph by Matthew Hall.

All inquiries should be made to the Publisher via sales@fairplaypublishing.com.au

 A catalogue record for this book is available from the National Library of Australia

Disclaimer

To the maximum extent permitted by law, the authors and publisher disclaim all responsibility and liability to any person, arising directly or indirectly from any person taking or not taking action based on the information in this publication.

ACKNOWLEDGEMENTS

Versions of some of these stories appeared in different formats in the pages of The *Guardian*, the *Observer*, the *Sydney Morning Herald*, *The Age*, *Rolling Stone*, *When Saturday Comes*, and *FourFourTwo*.

I'd like to thank the various editors over many years who agreed that there were stories to tell about Australian soccer that weren't being told properly – if at all.

Thanks especially to Tony Harper, James Carey (RIP), and Peter Gearin at Fairfax Media in Sydney; Mike Ticher and Andy Lyons at WSC; Elissa Blake and Andrew Humphreys at *Rolling Stone*; and Fairfax Media's lawyers who were always solid when things got interesting. Thanks to the coaches, players, and their families for giving their time; the agents and middlemen; federation and club officials; and the many sources with tips and information, many who needed to remain anonymous.

Thanks to Bonita Mersiades and the hardworking team at Fair Play Publishing for agreeing this was a great idea for a book.

ABOUT THE AUTHOR

Matthew Hall is the author of *The Away Game and Robbie Slater: The Hard Way*. He produced and wrote the award-winning film adaptation of The Away Game. He covered four FIFA World Cups while writing about football for The *Guardian*, the *Observer*, the *New York Times*, the *Sydney Morning Herald*, *The Age*, *The Sun-Herald*, *The Australian*, the *Daily Telegraph*, the *South China Morning Post*, *Rolling Stone*, *When Saturday Comes*, *FourFourTwo*, *Inside Sport*, *Playboy*, ESPN, *The World Game*, and the *Saturday Paper*, among others.

He has campaigned against human rights violations in sport and human trafficking through sports. Born in Perth, Western Australia, he lives in New York City where he coaches girls soccer teams.

CONTENTS

Introduction 1

If I started to cry, I wouldn't stop 3

Mark Bosnich leaves a message and wants to talk 6

Harry Kewell has a crocodile in his backyard 15

Croatia is a country 22

Into the weeds 31

Frank Farina: "That's not a bullshit answer." 46

Nicky Salapu can count to 57 50

A cauldron of hell with a bottle of wine 54

In Oceania, no one can hear you scream 58

Like their players, Australian agents taste the big time 61

The Invisible Man 64

In Japan, Ned Zelic misses Australia, but regrets nothing . 72

Terry Antonis is 10 years old but everything will come true ... 74

We have one car between us 76

Shiny and new: Frank Lowy dreams of Sydney, New Zealand, and Asia ... 79

That time Australian football was going to buy a Premier League club ... 82

Tim Cahill, "the situation", and his arrival in the Premier League ... 84

Johnny Warren, the beat of bossa nova, and saudade 88

Frank Farina fights fires
(and other part time jobs for a national team coach) 92

Harry Kewell prays he doesn't break down 104

Guus Hiddink with wind in his hair 107

Wide awake in Marrakech 109

Montevideo diary: "Goodbye, good luck, and well played." … 115

Fallen and forlorn, Harry Kewell rises again … 120

Andrew Jennings was right about everything … 128

No one can eat until Guus says so … 132

Don Parkes and the birthday present dream … 134

Herr Maisenbacher's tears are all of us … 137

The eternal search for the Next Big Thing … 140

At home against the mafia, match-fixing, and riots … 145

Graham Arnold and the drama queens … 147

A Galaxy with one star and the teammates just want dinner … 150

Some of them… they are going to be killed … 154

Fabio Capello is "added to the process" … 157

Mark Shield is a referee - and a human being … 163

Harry Kewell will arrive in precisely 13 minutes … 166

A dinner with Frank Lowy and Jack Warner … 169

I just want to be the person that I really was … 172

Clueless and the international man of mystery … 176

A photo from Jamaica raises quiet questions … 187

The best motorcycle mechanic in Dili … 190

The sun sets into the Meadowlands
(and no one sees Qatar coming) … 193

Beware of friends with private jets … 198

The footballers would head in one direction
and the soldiers take another to war … 201

Therapy … 206

INTRODUCTION

For almost 15 years I was a front row witness to what was happening in Australian football. I had little interest in what was taking place at the front of the stage, however. If this was a concert then my eyes were off the singer and I'd be watching the bass player, or the drummer, or the stage crew. I wanted to know what was happening behind the scenes or uncover the forgotten or untold stories that were – and are – important to documenting a social history.

For much of this time, getting an editor – even a sports editor - to take any interest in football was a battle. This was a time before Fox Sports, before the plethora of websites that exist now, before the internet. Not to sound too much like an old man dreaming of glorious and distant past but in the mid-1990s the only way to get overnight news from the Premier League on a Sunday morning was to dial a dollar-a-minute phone number where the late Les Murray would read out the scores at a snail's pace.

Media has changed since then and with that, much of Australian football's written history has been consigned to storage boxes or hidden parts of the internet. Part of the motivation for this book was to collect one version of that history – from the mid-90s to the mid-2010s – in one place. This book should not be seen as a complete history – far from it – but it is one perspective on the most tumultuous time in Australian football history.

I was lucky to be there when both Mark Bosnich and Harry Kewell were beginning their careers, when the National Soccer League was struggling to reinvent itself, when football's local administration was inept (this appears to be an ongoing issue), when Frank Lowy revealed his vision of the "future", when Australia qualified for the 2006 World Cup and when Australia was dumped out of that World Cup. Let's also not forget the bizarre and painful bid for the 2018 and 2022 World Cups which, in retrospect, was a metaphor for the end of an era. The rails came off in 2010 in more ways than one.

After Australia's exit from the 2006 World Cup against Italy, I headed to Berlin to wait for a phone call. Lucas Neill, who had made the tackle that tipped over Italy's Fabio Grosso, had been in contact and wanted to talk. I felt like a therapist to the fallen stars. I waited and waited – for days – in a hotel for the call. When it came through, Neill had a lot to say. Football is a game of emotion and Neill had much to share. A line from that conversation – 'If I started to cry, I wouldn't stop" – became the title for this book. It summed up how many of us feel about the experience of Australian soccer (personally, as a veteran of a decades-long name wars, 'soccer' and 'football' are interchangeable). It has taken us to the highest highs and, for several reasons and on many occasions, the lowest lows.

Here are some of those stories.

Matthew Hall
New York City
March, 2019

Note to readers

The governing body for association football in Australia has been known by several names in just a few decades. Those names include the Australian Soccer Federation, Soccer Australia, the Australian Soccer Association, and Football Federation Australia. This book uses the names in use at the time recounted.

IF I STARTED TO CRY, I WOULDN'T STOP

Berlin, July 2006

There were worse places to wait for three days for a call from Lucas Neill than an anonymous hotel on the outskirts of Berlin. There was a joke among some journalists who cover football that when asked to describe their job it was best summed up as hanging around in car parks waiting for young millionaires to finish their two-hour work day and then ignore your questions as they went home to their mansions to play video games.

So, Berlin for 72 hours waiting for a call was luxury - even if that call was from the Australian captain whose buzzkill tackle had sent Australia tumbling out of the World Cup. Neill was a savvy captain of the Australian team and could also be a charming host. He knew - without the benefit of advice from a PR representative - he had to speak about the game against Italy. "I'll call, I'll call," he said. And did. Devastation. Bitterness. Anger. Pride. Shock. Desire. Disappointment. He'd felt the spectrum of emotions since the 94th minute of Australia's final 2006 World Cup match. Sometimes, as some journalists know, you just press record on your tape machine and let someone unload. This was one of those times.

"I'm not over it yet," Neill said before boarding a flight from Europe to Australia. "For the rest of my life it will eat away at me that we had a realistic opportunity to get to the semi-final of the World Cup. We had everything under control in the game. We knew that, whether it be in extra time or on penalties, that we were going to beat a giant of world football. But it was all taken out of our control. I'm disappointed. I am gutted. Mentally, before the game, I thought that we were going to beat Italy. And then when we were playing the game, I knew we would. We were going to go on to bigger and better things. I might play in another World Cup but this squad will never ever be the same. The coach. The Guus factor. The team was very talented. There were so many great ingredients going into that team. We had momentum and great confidence. There was no expectation. We had the opportunity for more of a great adventure."

After being one of the outstanding players of the tournament, Neill's world caved in with just eight seconds of normal time remaining against Italy. The Azzurri, down to 10 men, had absorbed wave after wave of Australian attacks, and with the clock ticking, launched a desperate last attempt at Mark Schwarzer's goal. Fabio Grosso turned Mark Bresciano near the touch line and then headed towards the penalty area. Grosso had the ball at his feet. Neill was about to be mugged.

"I didn't even try to tackle the ball or the man," Neill recalled. "I just tried to block the possibility of him crossing it. He was not going to go anywhere. If he went back inside, he would have been pushed away from the goal. I can't be angry at the player because he is trying to do whatever he can to try and win the game for his country. I'm in too much shock to be angry at anyone in particular but, in hindsight, I wish I hadn't tried to be so cute and block the cross. I should have stayed on my feet and let him shoot or let him try and score from a ridiculous angle."

Asked if he blamed the referee for misjudging the incident, an emotional Neill paused before answering.

"That is not for me to say. I don't blame him. But I blame a wrong decision that has cost Australia, and everybody in the team, and me, everything. We have gone from a massive high to a massive low, based on one wrong decision that nobody will ever be able to do anything about and we couldn't react to because there was no time left in the game," he said. "I was still in shock straight after. On the field, I was holding back tears because I knew that if I started to cry, I wouldn't stop. I even shook hands with the ref and the Italians. I asked the ref to have a look at the decision on the TV so he would lose sleep at night and he promised that he would do that.

"Then I said to him that it is not going to change what happened and he said no, it wouldn't. I went into the dressing room and just wasn't. While 1996 may seem like a trip in a time machine, much of what Bosnich said was incisive at the time and still relevant today. He was a confident 24 years old and wiser and more self-aware than pretty much anyone of his age - or even older.

He explained that growing up in the western suburbs of Sydney as the son of immigrants who moved from Croatia to Australia in the late 1950s, he was tossed up whether to pursue his talents in cricket, rugby league, or his father's passion - soccer. Watching Craig Johnston lift the English FA Cup with Liverpool in 1985 made up his mind. Clutching a reference from a well-connected NSW team coach, he turned up for a trial at Liverpool Football Club on the tail end of a family holiday in Europe at the age of 15.

Liverpool were impressed and offered a contract but while Bosnich returned to Australia to finish school and finalise the deal, rivals Manchester United swooped and pinched him from Liverpool's grasp. What followed was a tough three-year course in soccer know-how with United until he was deported on the not inaccurate grounds he was keeping English goalkeepers from a job.

Back in Australia, boyhood friend and Sydney United understudy Zeljko Kalac had given such outstanding performances during Bosnich's absence from club duty with the Olympic team that, having faced the likes of Gary Lineker one week, Bosnich now found himself unable to hold down a place with his local side.

At rock bottom, for Bosnich the only way was up. He married his English girlfriend (and qualifying for British residency) bought out his contract with Sydney United and headed back to the UK, where he chose to sign with English dub Aston Villa over Scottish giants Glasgow Rangers. Ferguson was furious at his return to England with another club, a factor that would prove important - and fateful - in the future. But, four years later, having claimed two League Cup winners' medals with the Birmingham club, Bosnich was considered one of the best goalkeepers playing in Europe, if not the world. At the time I wrote, "Australia may soon be able to claim a genuine world soccer great as our own". I was right, but as we now know, the story would take some incredible twists. All that was to come later puts this conversation in an intriguing context.

Q: Why did you choose to be a goalkeeper?

A: I just wasn't good enough to play outfield. When you play five-a-side the worst player always ends up in goal. I used to play a lot of cricket and rugby league at school, so I was also good with my hands. Some people call goalkeeping "madness" but it's just more of a mind game - you are judged a lot on your split-second decisions.

Q: Do you recall your first team debut with Manchester United?

A: It was against Wimbledon at Old Trafford and I was taken totally by surprise when I was selected. I was very nervous. The next year I played two games - it was really nice being able to play three games for Manchester United, having been there for three years! I'd played through the youth teams, the A team, the reserves. I played at places you wouldn't even have heard of, on rainy Wednesday nights in snow or frost. It was a real education.

Q: Explain what it's like to face Jurgen Klinsmann or Eric Cantona, and the best players in the world, every week.

A: The funny things is that when I'm in Australia it seems a little more daunting and intimidating than it is is reality. The guys in Australia don't realise how good they really are but because we're so far away and only see those people on TV they become like demigods. But they're only human. Playing against Cantona and Klinsmann and people like Maradona, I could be playing against my dad's mates on Sunday and still get the same butterflies and the same nervous tension.

Q: Is the English Premier League the best in the world?

A: I would say without doubt it's the most entertaining. I think the Italian league is the best for quality and technique, simply because in the European competitions, recently, the Italians have done so well. I haven't played in the Italian league but entertainment wise there's nothing like English soccer. As far as exporting around the world, with TV rights, the only thing that compares is NBA basketball.

Q: How do you describe the intense passion that envelops the crowds at soccer matches?

A: This year I watched the State of Origin in Queensland. That means a lot to people there. Two-nil down in the series and 15-2 down in the game, they were still screaming for Queensland. If you can multiply the State of Origin by 10, then you get an idea of what the atmosphere at a European soccer match is like. Maybe that's why every major war in the last century has focused around Europe. Unfortunately, games in Australia like that have been tainted with ethnic rivalry which we could do without.

Q: So, you think the ethnic influence has thwarted the appeal of soccer with the general public in Australia?

A: Yes. In the past, petty politics played too much of a part in Australian soccer. It's about time we started thinking big time. I might get lynched by the Croatian community for saying this but the most important thing is to Australianise the game. I have an English fiancée but I can't take her to a Croatia (Sydney United) game and make her feel welcome. You go to UTS Olympic or Marconi and it's the same. It's fine to be proud of where your parents hail from but we now live in Australia, okay? We are Australian. Why is it so important to wave a Croatian or Greek flag at a game? If it is that important, go back to the country that your parents are from and do it there. They are keeping so many people away. Do you feel more comfortable taking your family to see Eastern Suburbs at the Sydney Football Stadium or going to see UTS Olympic versus Sydney Croatia? Even if you hate rugby league, where are you going to spend your money? You could talk to 100 people in Sydney and about 70 to 80 would go to a rugby league game. I feel sorry for the Australian soccer fans, I really do. I feel a little awkward that they can't come and watch. There are so many people that we are denying the game.

Q: What advantages does soccer have over the other codes in Australia?

A: One advantage is that we are a true world game. No disrespect to all the other codes - it's a fact. The others are very, very, limited and regionalised. The Super 12 concept is great, but rugby union has only a few Test playing nations. Aussie rules, well, there's no other country in the world who plays it. Rugby league, sure, the last two Test series against Britain have been closely run, but we still won with our second-choice team and no other Test playing nation has given Australia a true run. Nobody. When the big soccer tournaments are on, or an FA Cup night, how many people around Australia are interested? A lot, right? You're not going to tell me they are rugby league fans. They're true football supporters. The problem is that they can't identify with a team in Australia and have no one to follow.

Q: Did you have much involvement with the Stewart inquiry?

A: I read about it but I still don't know enough to form an educated opinion. The most pointed bit about the whole thing was it was all so negative but the people involved were all exonerated. Allegations were made but they stank of jealousy. One point that sticks in my mind was the barbecue we were supposed to have with the Olympic team in Papendaal. I mean, how petty can you get?

Q: You mean the now infamous barbecue in Holland prior to the 1992 Olympic Games where it was suggested that Eddie Thomson had invited agents to meet players in a sort of "meat market"?

A: Yeah, and that was ludicrous. I was at that barbecue and, yes, there were agents present. One was my agent - who I invited. I know my agent wanted to come and see me and I said, "Come down to Papendaal." He asked if it would be okay and we had to check it with the Australian Soccer Federation. Eddie Thomson said, sure, bring your friends. There were a couple of the other boys' agents who were invited down, too. There was nothing sinister whatsoever.

Q: Is Eddie Thomson respected by the players?

A: Oh, very much so. If you have any type of problem, personal or other, he's always there. He is one of the best coaches I've worked with. We got enough stories in Scotland when the Australian team played in Glasgow earlier this year about how much of a legend he supposedly is there! Alex Ferguson went to school with him and they know each other like that. He worked professionally with Brian Little and Ron Atkinson at Aston Villa and Ferguson at Manchester United and I'd put Eddie Thomson in that group. I don't want to sound sucky or that I'm one of his boys - I'm just telling the truth. He's definitely a player's manager. But if he joins in a five-a- side game at training, I'll still kick him!

Q: There has been criticism leveled at national selection policies - no one seems to know who the Socceroos are at the moment.

A: Fair enough comment. But the same situation happened with England recently, too. Australia has so much time between World Cups. We don't have a tournament every two years like the Europeans and South Americans. We only have one every four years. It would be nice to play in an Asian nations cup, so we could have that competition between World Cups, but at the moment there's nothing going in that scene. In the interim, Eddie Thomson has to experiment. In the friendly games the result isn't as important as watching and learning things about your own players. World Cup time is result time.

Q: Australia hasn't qualified for the World Cup finals since 1974. We've regularly missed out since by the odd goal. How will we go for 1998 in France?

A: I truly believe that if we don't qualify this time we need shooting. Not the coach or the administration but the players. We're the ones who are going to make or break Australian soccer's reputation. We've been handed an easy draw that means we have to qualify through Asia. It's a draw that, in comparison to playing an Argentina or Scotland, is a little bit more accommodating. But then again, going to places like Uzbekistan or China can be even more testing.

Q: Australia rates at about 50 in the FIFA world rankings. How do you rate us?

A: Skill-wise, we compare with Asia and definitely with the African nations and some of the lesser European nations. But we're not far off the top echelon of Brazil, Argentina, Italy and Germany. Those teams may beat us seven times out of 10 but we can compete with them. The inroads Australian soccer has made internationally is amazing. People can't believe the players that we are producing. Ten years ago, they would say, "Jesus Christ, Aussie, kangaroo". But now because of people like Craig Johnston, Paul Okon, and Aurelio Vidmar, they take us seriously. If we keep progressing the way we are going, we should compare ourselves with the best and shouldn't settle for anything less than the best.

Q: You controversially "retired" from international football just before the climax of the 1994 World Cup qualifiers and didn't play against Canada. What was the story behind that?

A: At 21 I'd just broken into the Aston Villa side but I still had a huge challenge coming from Nigel Spink [the veteran Villa goalkeeper whom Bosnich had unseated]. The stakes were very, very, high. On the other hand, the Australian team, who I love, had the games against Canada. My offer was to play in Canada and do the business there so that I wouldn't have to play in the second game and therefore be able to play for Aston Villa. But it would set a precedent - which I can understand - for players to take it upon themselves to not play specific games and to pick and choose their availability.

Q: Why was it necessary to so drastically "retire"?

A: I didn't want to retire - I just didn't want to be available for that second game in Sydney. The dates had been prearranged but they hadn't taken into consideration that players had to be in two places at the same time - the start of the English season was the same day. Retiring was a technical thing so that next time an international match came up FIFA wouldn't be able to suspend me from any corresponding games. At that time, I took legal advice and that was what it came to. At this stage, my livelihood was not secure. Now, it's a different story. I regret it and I'm sorry if I upset anyone, if they thought differently of me, if they thought I was sacrificing my country for the club.

Q: For a lot of Australians performing in overseas leagues, not just in soccer, but Luc Longley with the Chicago Bulls in the NBA, too, club versus country is a tough issue, isn't it?

A: Unfortunately, playing for Australia doesn't, and shouldn't pay for my lifestyle. But Aston Villa Football Club does. If I upset the club too much that's one thing. On the other hand, there is the prestige and commitment to the national team. I've been playing in the Villa first team for three years now and I can sit back and say that in a couple of years' time - if everything goes to plan - I won't have to work after I'm 35. But at that time, it wasn't like that. In the end though, I was the only loser, because Australia won against Canada and I lost my place at Villa through suspension for the first seven games of the season.

Q: Would you consider the subsequent World Cup game in Sydney against Argentina as your biggest match? [Bosnich declared himself eligible to play against [Argentina] unseating Mark Schwarzer, a penalty shoot-out hero against Canada].

A: It ranks up there. The game against Argentina captured the nation's hearts and minds. I remember even Madonna wore an Australian shirt at a concert just after. There was the game versus Portugal at the Youth World Cup in 91, in front of 120,000 people, that was special, too. My debut with the Manchester United first team is another one. And later, playing with Aston Villa against Manchester United at Old Trafford when we were both going for the title was big. I put in a virtuoso display that made my name. I got a lot of abuse that they reserve only for special players. That was a real compliment! My UEFA Cup debut against the Spanish team Deportivo La Coruna where I saved a penalty against Bebeto was great.

Q: As a goalkeeper, what was your take on FIFA's suggestion to widen the goals?

A: I wouldn't mind that at all. If widening the goals improves the game, so be it. Football is about goals, not about goalkeepers saving them. It would sort out the average goalies from the great ones! If it makes it a more entertaining game and people come and watch, that's good. Look at the back-pass rule. Everyone turned their nose up at that but it's turned it into a faster game.

Q: So, do you have three wishes for Australian soccer?

A: Quite importantly, that we qualify for the next World Cup. Secondly, that in the foreseeable future we establish a professional league in Australia. Thirdly, and most important in the overall sense, is that everyone involved in Australian soccer pulls the rope in the same direction. I said it earlier and I'll say it again - put aside the petty rivalries and jealousies. If people can't do that, they should get out. Soccer is going places. Put aside everything for the common goal.

Q: You're only 24 and you have three years left on your contract with Aston Villa. Where do you see yourself heading at the end of that?

A: Parramatta Rugby League Club! My boyhood heroes. I said that to Peter Sterling when I met him in Sydney this year and he couldn't believe it. Peter Sterling! Brett Kenny! Mark Bosnich! I'd like to see that!

HARRY KEWELL HAS A CROCODILE IN HIS BACKYARD

Leeds, January 1999

Harry Kewell has had a good winter. He regained the form that made him such a mouthwatering prospect last spring, his Leeds United team have become everybody's second favourite team and - as if that wasn't enough - every morning he woke up to good news.

"While the Ashes were on in Australia I always clicked on the telly in the morning to see how it was going," he says.

How it was going, of course, was that Australia was handing England their ritual stuffing. Kewell, like every good Australian, was always able to find a Pom with whom to share his team's last triumph.

"I talk to [Leeds United] Nigel Martyn about cricket - he loves it," Kewell says, which suggests that the Leeds keeper's winter was a long and depressing one.

That Kewell, an outstanding young Australian sportsman, should be enjoying an Ashes series on the other side of the world, while playing professional football in England, is a telling indication of the changing sporting landscape down under. Australia has traditionally produced brilliant cricketers and rugby players by the bar-load, not to mention more than its fair share of outstanding swimmers and tennis players, but decent Australian footballers have been a rarity - until recently.

Now, as well as Kewell, there are a handful of Premiership goalkeepers (including Aston Villa's much-coveted Mark Bosnich), West Ham's highly rated wing-back Stan Lazaridis, not to mention one of Europe's deadliest strikers. Lazio's Christian Vieri may be an Italian international, but he spent much of his childhood in Australia and speaks English with an authentic Aussie twang. All of them, like Kewell, have forsaken traditional Australian sporting careers and opted instead for the world game.

"I was pretty good at backyard cricket, you know, with a rubbish bin for stumps," Kewell says with a grin. "I'm like Steve Waugh - a bit of an all-rounder. I can bowl, bat, field".

And it wasn't just cricket. As a kid growing up in the outskirts of Sydney, Kewell could hold his own in many sports. "I played rugby league at school just to see what it was like. Everyone in Australia always plays different sports. They go out and try different things."

But it was football Kewell chose. It was in his blood. From the age of five, when he first saw English football matches on TV (his favourite teams were Liverpool and Chelsea), the young Kewell decided he wanted to become a footballer. Not every Australian youngster was making the same decision. A few years earlier in another Sydney suburb - at a time when Kewell thought dribbling was away to pass the time rather than something to do with a ball - two 14-year-olds were making a difficult decision. They'd been selected to play schoolboy football for Australia but weren't sure whether it was time to concentrate on their other sport. A generation of English cricketers have lived to rue the day Mark and Steve Waugh decided the game of Don Bradman and Richie Benaud offered far better career possibilities.

Not that Kewell's decision to choose football should come as much of a surprise. Even at primary school he showed outstanding potential as a footballer.

"I first spotted Harry when he was in a primary school rep team," says David Lee, then Director of Coaching at the New South Wales Soccer Academy. "Harry was probably just a little bit better than most but they were an outstanding side."

Kewell's talent won him places at the NSW Academy - one of several regional centres across Australia for talented young footballers - and also Westfield Sports High, a government school for gifted athletes. By the age of 16 he was receiving rave reviews as a member of the national under-17 side and it was then that he received his big break - a scholarship for trials with a club in England.

"It's called the Big Brother movement," explains Lee. "It used to fund people to come from England to Australia to better themselves: kids who were orphans or looking for jobs. It now funds people who'd benefit from going to Britain for a while - artists, piano players - or footballers."

But Leeds United wasn't singled out for special attention. Indeed, the story of how the Yorkshire club acquired Kewell - a player they could sell tomorrow for millions - may act as a reminder to all football clubs that it pays to keep up with the paperwork.

"We'd write to 60 English clubs and if 15 replied with an answer, even if that answer was that they weren't interested, we'd be doing well," recalls Lee. "They're mostly hopeless. Up until 12 months ago, Crystal Palace used to answer letters with just a scribble.

Leeds, though, made the effort, and invited the 17-year-old Kewell over on trial along with another hopeful called Brett Emerton.

"We knew when Harry got here that he had a lot of ability,' says Eddie Gray, Leeds United's assistant coach. 'He was a bit quiet for the first two weeks but after that he was fine. He has a lot of confidence in himself."

Whatever Harry Kewell achieves with Leeds, it is unlikely that he will score a goal that will have a greater effect on a crowd than the one he notched for Australia in November 1997. It came on a Saturday night in Tehran as the Aussies took on Iran in a World Cup qualifier - with the winner going to France 98, the loser consigned to oblivion. Kewell remembers the moment well. The ball was flicked on by Mark Viduka and - bang! - he has crashed it into the back of the net. Suddenly 110,000 Iranians went very, very, quiet.

"It was great," Kewell says of the silence that filled the Azadi stadium. "You feel like you've really done something. The crowd was devastated, but only for about ten seconds. Then they started up again - the noise was incredible. I was trying to speak to someone about ten metres away. I was yelling and yelling but they couldn't hear me. I had to run up and tap them on the shoulder."

Kewell's place in the starting line-up in. Tehran was a surprise to pretty much everyone. Although he had made his debut for the Socceroos in a 1996 friendly against Chile (before he'd played a hill game for the Leeds United first team), the decision of Australia coach Terry Venables to pick him for such a crucial game caused a considerable stir because he hadn't been a regular. Venables, on the advice of his old friend George Graham (then the Leeds United boss) had given Kewell 45 minutes in a friendly just before the game with Iran - a 3-0 win over Tunisia. Even so, Kewell's selection for the Tehran game sent Australian officials scrambling to find a photo for publicity purposes. The best they could find was one of Kewell as a mullet-haired 15-year-old.

"I didn't think I'd get picked," says Kewell. "I was definitely the dark horse but that's the way I like it - to come from nowhere."

The Tehran game ended 1-1, leaving the second leg wide open. A week later at the Melbourne Cricket Ground, Kewell could be found dancing in a corner of the pitch, swinging his hips and miming a celebratory song, a comer flag acting. as an imaginary microphone. He had put the Australians ahead and France beckoned. The 95,000 Australians at the MCG were going very, very, wild. With 13 minutes to go the Socceroos were two up, but a couple of late goals not only brought the Iranians level but sent them through on away goals. After a campaign in which they never lost a game and had a goal difference of plus-29, Australia were out. Kewell would not be going to the World Cup finals.

"The result against Iran was horrible but I loved every minute of that game at the MCG," he says. "Anyone representing their country should be very proud. I'm always proud to put on the Australian jersey."

But, Kewell's desire to pull on his country's colours has caused problems back in Yorkshire. Regarded in his homeland in much the same way as Michael Owen is in England, Kewell was called up to play in a tournament between Australia and Brazil's Olympic teams last March. Leeds were far from happy at the timing. In the event, the day before he was due to fly to Australia Kewell was injured. A fax war between club and country ensued with Australia asking FIFA to ban Kewell from playing for Leeds until the tournament was completed. As things turned out, Australia disposed of Brazil without Kewell's assistance, but relations between Leeds and Australia seemed irretrievably damaged.

"We want him to play for his country but it would probably have been a lot better for us if Harry hadn't played for Australia before he came here,' says Andy Gray. "Then he would have ended up playing for England."

Kewell, who has an English-born father and Australian mother, admits: "When I was little, playing in the park, I used to pretend I was Paul Gascoigne, playing for England."

But he adds a firm rejoinder: "Australia is my country. It is where I was born. When I put on that Australian shirt, that's it."

Leeds United's experience with Kewell has caused the club to change its attitude to the signing of youngsters from Australia. They will continue to do so and have entered into formal arrangements with the Westfield school and a junior club in Perth to act as feeders. The club has signed two players through their programs: 16-year-old Jamie McMaster and 14-year-old Matthew Hunter. But there is a condition: the youngsters must have British ancestry and renounce any claim to play for Australia.

"If, in eight years' time, we get four or five in our first team and they have to go backwards and forwards to play for Australia, then we're going to be short of first-team players,' says Alan Hill, director of Leeds United's Youth Academy. "It is important that the boys who come over decide they want to play for England, Ireland, Scotland or Wales rather than Australia."

Not surprisingly, the Australians are furious. "They're talking to players as young as 13, 14, 15 and there is no need to do that at such a young age," says Les Scheinflug, national coach of Australia's youth teams. "We have an excellent youth system here. FIFA acknowledges it as one of the best in the world. I've nothing against player going to

Europe when they are older but they don't have to go over so young."

David Lee, who oversaw Kewell's fledgling career in Sydney, agrees with Scheinflug but suspects the money at English clubs will outweigh the principle. "We can't compete with English wages," he says. 'You would struggle to get in a year in Australia what you can get in a week in England."

The next big date for Australia is the football at the Sydney Olympics. While many in Britain regard that competition as something between a joke and an irrelevance, the Australians are one of many countries taking it very seriously.

"Historically, the Olympics is important to Australia, it always has been," says Raul Blanco, Australia's Olympic coach. "I have 15 players lined up for the Olympic squad who play in Belgium, Holland, England, Greece, Japan and Italy. It is a difficult job because Australia is shown a lot of disrespect. Several countries are complacent in their attitude towards us. But that's OK. We will surprise a few people - again."

When asked why the 2000 Olympic Games is so important to him and his country, Kewell states simply: "The Olympics is in Australia, isn't it? You're telling me you wouldn't want to have a gold medal from the Olympics sitting at home? A medal which would last for generations? Nope. There's no way anyone could not want that."

Still, Kewell is enjoying himself at Leeds. On the pitch he is, at *the age* of 20, an automatic selection in a team that has a growing reputation for its mixture of power, pace, and panache. Playing upfront, just behind the central strikers, or down the flank, he can usually be relied upon to produce a defence-unlocking moment, especially given his remarkable eye for an opening.

It is all a far cry from Smithfield, the south-west Sydney suburb where Kewell grew up. In good traffic it's about-90 minutes from the surf of Bondi Beach. Someone in the neighbourhood should think about printing postcards, though, because Smithfield and the next-door suburbs of Bossley Park and Fairfield have probably contributed more footballers to the world's top leagues than any comparable area on earth. Kewell, Bosnich, Middlesbrough's Mark

Schwarzer, plus Vieri and his Lazio team-mate Paul Okon, all played in the area as youngsters.

Not that many in the UK give much credence to Kewell when he talks about his roots. "People here think Australia is just like Neighbours and Home and Away, he says, referencing the Australian soap operas. "I don't know where they got that idea from. It's nice and peaceful there, fair enough, and everyone is very friendly, but I've never seen Billy Kennedy walking along the street."

"Some people have asked me if kangaroos and koalas walk down the street," he pauses. "Of course, I say yes. We have crocodiles in the backyard, too."

CROATIA IS A COUNTRY

Sydney/Zagreb 1999

It might be a muggy, wet, January Sunday afternoon in Sydney but the 30 or so Perth Glory fans, having traipsed across the continent to watch a game of soccer, are ecstatic. They're tumbling down the back stairs of Parramatta Stadium in Sydney relieved that their team has escaped with a 0-0 draw against league leaders Sydney United. Laughing and singing, they edge their way towards an exit: "Let's all have a disco... tra-la-la-la!"

Just outside the exit another group gathers, like storm clouds. These boys are big. And they're angry. To them, this travelling carnival of interloping good-time Western Australians has started to get very annoying. They strike up their own song but it has a different beat to the Perth fans' playful tune: "Fuck off, Glory! Fuck off, Glory!" The words are spat out and delivered with red-faced hard stares. A group of 30 or so angry men can make a lot of noise.

The Glory supporters stumble to a stop and suck in the sight. What was playful and teasing rivalry now takes a sinister twist. The already balmy atmosphere rises several degrees. The Sydney United boys, dressed in the red and white colours of their team, now take up a deep, guttural, mantra. The beat sways. There's a pause between every syllable. A grunt for the last.

The chant goes: "CROW-AH-TZEE-UH! CROW-AH-TZEE-UH!"

A tight pack forms and shuffles forward, slowly edging toward the Perth supporters, now trapped in a no-fans-land between the stadium fence and the straining faces of this angry chanting throng: "CROW-AH-TZEE-UH! CROW-AH-TZEE-UH!"

"What are they chanting?" a bystander asks a nervous security guard.

"Croatia," the security guard answers, now looking around for some assistance.

"Oh," says the first guy, not quite satisfied with the answer.

The scene seems set to explode. A presenter from a well-known TV soccer program scuttles around the edge of the growing crowd of onlookers. He mills about for a few seconds checking out the brewing action before scooting off in the direction of a car park. Finally, at last, police arrive and move both sets of supporters in opposite directions. Incident diffused but the Sydney United fans, now joined by blokes over 50 years-old, younger kids, and red-faced teenagers, shuffle off towards Parramatta's city centre. They're defiant to the last. Their fists in the air they once again begin their chant:

"CROW-AH-TZEE-UH! CROW-AH-TZEE-UH!"

Welcome to soccer - the world game - Australian style.

"OOH, OOH, USTASHA! OOH, OOH, USTASHA!"

CHANT AT PARRAMATTA STADIUM, JANUARY 18, 1998

The events at Parramatta registered as the most minorest of minor blips in the history of Sydney United fans. The season before last, another game was held at Parramatta, this time against local rivals Marconi, a club with strong ties to Western Sydney's immigrant Italian community. After that match, groups of young guys, some wearing Croatia soccer tops or t-shirts with the slogan "Croatian Nationalist League", harangued female Marconi supporters as they left the stadium. "What you need is a big cock up your arse!" was one choice piece of unsolicited advice given to the Marconi girls.

In the car park, a group of about 20 guys chased two or three others through the line of exiting cars and up on to a grassy bank by the Parramatta leagues club. They were caught and kicked and punched to the ground. As this was happening, the rest of the mob chanted "Croatia!"

Said the duty officer at Parramatta police station afterwards: "There were no arrests, so it was a pretty quiet night."

In May 1997, things came to an ugly climax at yet another Sydney United match when supporters spilled on to the Parramatta pitch at full-time and ended up exchanging blows with rival fans of

South Melbourne, a club with strong links to Melbourne's Greek community, as well as fighting security staff, and police. That blow up came as no real surprise to wide-eyed observers of the game in Australia. However, this time, the incident was escalated after players became involved in the violence and news photographers and TV cameramen were punched and kicked - some had their equipment damaged. For the next 24 hours, pictures of the incident were splashed across newspapers and TV (this was before the days of ubiquitous social media).

That fracas sparked a furious media frenzy that lasted weeks. The hot issue was about so-called "ethnic rivalry" between fans played out at soccer games. The "ethnic" teams were a platform for hatred, according to many commentators. The violence was, according to one nationally syndicated columnist, downright "un-Australian". Soccer Australia, the game's local governing body that oversaw the league, suggested Sydney United may be "kicked out" of the national league because of its fans behaviour, a couple of whom ended up in jail for offences connected with events that day.

Ultimately, after a vicious legal battle that co-opted not only the Supreme Court but also FIFA, the club could stay, instead receiving a heavy fine for its penance. Everyone had an opinion on the issue. Everyone had a say. Everyone, that is, except for the fans - the people supposedly causing the trouble.

"KING TOM! KING TOM! KING TOM! KING TOM!"

CHANT AT PARRAMATTA STADIUM, JANUARY 11, 1998

The King Tomislav Croatian Club is located at Edensor Park in Sydney's west. In the late 90s, you couldn't drive any further in Sydney. Well, you could, but the next suburb was a farm. "King Tom" was the home ground for Sydney United until the team was forced to move to Parramatta as one of Soccer Australia's conditions for the team staying in the national competition. The stadium shift was designed to literally move the team away from its Croatian roots and "broaden its support base". Other directives included the introduction of a membership policy to counter the public perception that United were "an exclusive Croatian entity", as well as "aggressive recruitment of non-Croatian background players". In 1998 and 1999, the King Tom stadium now sat idle, though back when they had match days it was buzzing. Croatian newspapers, cassettes, and videos were on sale and fruit and hams were sold off the back of trucks. It was just like market day in downtown Zagreb.

Inside King Tom the walls were adorned with portraits of King Tomislav, the guy behind the first Croatian state way back in 925 AD. There are maps and photos of Croatia, old blokes sat around drinking coffee and beer and playing chess. In the main auditorium, young kids, aged about five and dressed in oversized Croatia soccer shirts, learned folk dances alongside teenage girls, one who wore a tight t-shirt with a "Fuct" logo on the front. You rebel any way you can here. But everyone still sings Advance Australia Fair together at the end of the dance class.

In the front bar, the VBs are on Tony. Along with his mate Joe and another guy, Tony #2, all in their mid-20s, they were part of Sydney United's hardcore support, the Bad Blue Boys (BBB) for most of the 1990s. In their prime, the Sydney BBB were very badly-behaved boys. They took their lead from the supporters of Dinamo Zagreb, one of the former-Yugoslavia's most famous football teams. In 1989, the Zagreb BBB were involved in one of the most notorious incidents of football hooliganism, ever. A clash with Red Star Belgrade supporters, considered the "government team", ended in a huge riot.

In one infamous moment, Dinamo Zagreb player Zvonimir Boban, who would later become a huge star with the Croatian national side, joined the ruckus by attacking police with a kung-fu kick and saving a Dinamo fan by being beaten by the cops. Clashes took place around the city long into the night. Guns were fired. Hospitals filled injured fans. Some people consider the riot to be the spark of the Yugoslav civil war. So compared with their Zagreb cousins, Sydney's BBB are a bunch of fluffy kittens.

"This 'ethnic rivalry' that people here go on about is bullshit," says Tony of the fights in Australia. "It's not 'ethnic' violence. It's just plain old violence. Croatians don't have anything against Greeks or Italians. There are fights at the cricket between different people. But what's that? Is that ever reported as ethnic violence?"

"JINGLE BELLS, JINGLE BELLS, BAD BLUE BOYS ARE HERE! WE'RE HERE TO FUCK YOUR WOMEN AND DRINK UP ALL YOUR BEER!"
CHANT AT EDENSOR PARK, 1994

Dr John Hughson, an ethnologist at the University of New England at Armidale, NSW, spent two seasons with Sydney's BBB. He listened to them sing songs celebrating the Ustasha, the Croatian secret police responsible for holocaust-like atrocities during World War Two. He travelled with them and saw them fight in Melbourne. He drank with them. He stood next to them when they wore t-shirts idolising Ante Pavelic, the Nazi collaborator who led Croatia during the 1940s.

Still, he believes nothing too hardcore should be read into the political posturing. They're just boys, he reckons. Rebels with a hazy cause. First-and second-generation Australians with a chip on their shoulder. Disenfranchised? Alienated from the rest of society? Identity crisis? Get in the van. The soccer matches are just a backdrop for a lot of confused, contradictory malarkey.

Hughson studied the BBB for his PhD at a unique time. The war in Europe was all the rage. Soccer Australia was making one of its several moves to outlaw any Australian soccer club having an "ethnic" name - the mantra was that if clubs wanted to be in a national league and attract crowds, they had to appeal to mainstream Australia. From 1958 until 1992 the club was called Sydney Croatia but for the club - and the professional sport - to grow, the brains at Soccer HQ said that had to change.

"We didn't want change but if everyone else was going to then we'd do it," recalls Tony. Sydney United's local rivals Marconi, however, changed nothing. That club's argument was that "Marconi" was neither an ethnic name nor nationalistic. Conspiracy theories? Fox Mulder plays centre-forward for Sydney United.

"You're trying to tell me Marconi isn't an ethnic name?" asks Tony.

"Croatians are useless at organising and don't know how PR works," adds Tony #2 of the bad media attention the club received. He points across the room at the old men playing chess. "These guys are bricklayers and farmers. If the press ring up they'll say anything. They're not businessmen like the Greeks and Italians. We don't know how to sweet talk the media and do deals like those guys do. The other clubs have got away with everything they've done but because we're the poorest club and we're the easiest target, we cop it."

The name change from "Croatia" to "United" didn't bring the desired hordes through the turnstiles. In 1996, as part of yet another attempted marketing push, Soccer Australia demanded clubs drop "ethnic" logos. Sydney United was forced to alter their badge from a traditional Croatian shield. Other clubs were forced to change too - minimally. Attendance figures remained unaffected.

"The oldies are tired," says Joe at the King Tom Club. The fines, the struggle over identity, the trouble, has taken its toll. "They're fed up with the soccer club and want to put their money into a retirement home being set up by the local church."

Last season the BBB got tired too. They saw the club that once stood for what they believed - their very own heritage - being taken away from them. Add pressure from club officials and concern from family members over some of their more extreme behaviour and the hardcore dropped off.

"We've stopped going to games, now," says Joe. "If we were playing at Edensor Park maybe we'd go but at Parramatta they body search us before we go in. It's all too much hassle."

The torch has been handed to a younger, smaller, group. The ones who continued to stir things up. The group that now causes the club an image problem and Soccer Australia many headaches. The group that has a mass of security on its shoulder at every home game.

"It's quite funny," says Joe. "It's only 15 to 20 kids causing trouble. Yet they bring so much attention to themselves and are responsible for this huge security presence. How the fuck Sydney United and

Soccer Australia can't control them is beyond me."

"AUSSIE! AUSSIE! AUSSIE! OI! OI! OI!"

MAKSIMIR STADIUM, ZAGREB,

JUNE 6, 1998

You feel at home at Zagreb's Maksimir stadium. Not just because of the summer heat but the locals dress much the same way as they do at Parramatta Stadium on a Sunday. Croatia and Dinamo Zagreb shirts are the rage. The difference on this June day is that among the crowd are three Perth Glory Fans (who seem to travel everywhere), a Carlton supporter, two Sydney United fans, and a clutch of Socceroo shirts. You don't even get that at Parramatta.

Croatia were off to the World Cup on the Tuesday after the game but on this day they host Australia for their last warm-up match. The Australian support is made up of a couple of cashed-up oldies on their way to watch the World Cup in France, some have-a-go backpackers, and a few Australians doing a year's work in their parent's old hometown. The Australian selection is an ad-hoc team, devoid of nearly all first - even second choice - stars so it's no surprise that Croatia run rings around these Socceroos. The most significant issue the match raises is that the promising player Anthony Seric, formerly of the Sydney suburb of Hurstville and a product of the prestigious government-funded Australian Institute of Sport, makes his second-ever appearance on the international stage for Croatia.

After the one-sided match (Croatia won 7-0), people gather in bars across from the stadium to drink away the dusty Zagreb heat. "II don't know why we played that game," says one Australian supporter wearing a Sydney United shirt. "It's not a result that will do us any good."

A group of Australians sullenly nod their heads in agreement.

"A win like that might affect our morale the wrong way," continues the Sydneysider, having mistakenly made everyone think he was speaking about the Socceroos. "Now we'll go off to the World Cup and think that we can win the thing."

Goran, who has been living and working in Zagreb for nine months, raises his head from his beer and shakes his head and breathes out: "Jesus, sometimes I can't wait to get back to Sydney…"

(Croatia would go on to reach the semi-finals of the 1998 World Cup).

"WE ARE RED, BLUE AND WHITE, WE ARE FUCKING DYNAMITE!"

PARRAMATTA STADIUM,

JANUARY 11, 1998

The week after the Perth Glory showdown is game two in an advertised "blockbuster Awesome Foursome" series of home games for Sydney United. The run of games is a marketing initiative to get Joe Aussie and his family out to Parramatta to watch "the team for Sydney". Yet despite Sydney United's runaway success on the field, the crowds are again down this year. Still, groups of young men, all dressed up in Croatia or Dinamo shirts hang around. Gaggles of old men chatter away in Croatian. Young women, some with dyed red or green hair and wearing t-shirts of the rock band Pennywise arrive with their mothers.

Inside the stadium, at the front of one of the main stands and directly in front of the stadium's private boxes, sit a group of about 20 guys. They're the ringleaders from last week's stoush. This week, though, they're fairly laid back save for the occasional howl for "Croatia!" that fails to get adopted by anyone else in the crowd. It's not all benign. Every time a Black player on the other team touches the ball, they shout "Nigger!".

As the game draws to a close it's decided that it's time to start some louder noise. But not for these guys a chant of "United!" nor a stirring, call for "Sydney" despite the best efforts of marketing departments. As one supporter cold John Hughson: "They can make as many rules as they like but they can't stop us. They can stop the club from calling itself Croatia but they can't stop Sydney United From being a Croatian club. It's always up to the supporters just what a club stands for."

The new next generation of Sydney United fans rise to their feet.

"MI HRAVATI! MI HRAVATI!" they roar.

They raise their arms in a Nazi-style salute.

"MI HRAVATI! MI HRAVATI!"

The chant booms around the cavernous stands, made even more noticeable by the smwall crowd of a few thousand spectators.

From the pitch, a Sydney United player called Velimir Kupresak acknowledges the chant with a wave.

Egged on, the fans continue to chant:

"MI HRAVATI! MI HRAVATI!"

They're singing: *"We are Croatian! We are Croatian!"*

These boys know exactly what the club stands for.

* Some names have been changed.

INTO THE WEEDS

Sydney, 1999

I'd met Paul Okon, one of Australia's best players and at the time a future captain of Australia, in Rome when he was playing for Lazio and asked if he was perturbed that his name would forever be linked with one of the most notorious scandals in Australian football. Despite no personal culpability in any of the alleged wrongdoings raised by the 1994 Stewart Report, Okon was a central figure in an affair that highlighted how the transfer of young Australian players to European clubs at the time was anarchic at best and corrupt at worst.

"There was a real dirty battle during those few years when players were [first] leaving Australia," he explained. "No one in Australia was used to the sort of money involved. My transfer was the opportunity to discover a lot of other things that went on that shouldn't have gone on."

The 'Okon transfer' was among the many subjects scrutinised in the now infamous Stewart Report. This was an investigation by Donald Stewart, an ex-High Court judge and former head of the National Crime Authority, at the behest of the Australian Soccer Federation. Its primary purpose was to look at the controversial transfers of several Australian players to overseas clubs. It involved high profile soccer figures such as coaches Eddie Thomson and Les Scheinflug, players Ned Zelic and Frank Farina and administrator Basil Scarsella, among many others.

However, the transfer of Paul Okon received more focus than any other transfer under Stewart's microscope owing to the complicated and mysterious nature of the deal. The transfer was highlighted in a report on ABC-TVs highly respected current affairs program, Four Corners. The Australian Soccer Federation, later known as Soccer Australia, was prompted to act after allegations and rumours that corruption was rife within the sport. Stewart eventually revealed that some of those allegations and rumours had basis in fact. Soccer was riddled with dishonesty, deceit, and a conspiracy of silence or, as the Italians call it, omerta.

The report tarnished the local game's reputation. Its findings were splashed across the front and back pages of newspapers around the country, prompting the national administrators to promise changes throughout all levels of the game. It also provoked wildly different reactions in the Australian soccer community. Some quarters, such as the media, players and fans, demanded sweeping changes to the national administration, to clean up the mess and make a fresh start, while others, including figures named in the report, downplayed the allegations, even laughed at them, ridiculing Stewart and his evidence. Alliances were made. Lifelong friendships were lost. It was a most public bloodletting.

"You can look in the dictionary and see what 'friendship' means and what 'friends' mean," said Okon when I'd asked if the Stewart Report's findings had tested his own friendships and allegiances. "It is completely different to what it means in real life. To me, friendship is my brother, my mother and my father. For the rest, there is no friendship." In other words, Okon was suggesting that these days he trusted no one.

The Okon family's history is entwined with that of Club Marconi, a casino-like social club in south-west Sydney. The family home was just one kilometre from the club. Like his sons, Klaus Okon Snr played for Marconi's football team. Paul Okon's grandfather was responsible for putting up the ground's first floodlights. Paul's uncles are builders who have carried out work at the club. Everyone knows each other. It could be said the club's community is not unlike a small European village with the club's main auditorium as its own square. Cleo Okon, Paul's mother, once even went so far as to say that, although not related by blood, the relationship between her family and that of Tony Labbozzetta, Marcon's one-time president, was just like family.

When Paul and Klaus Junior were kids, they regularly attended

NSL matches at Marconi's home ground. They would stand behind a goal, their faces painted in club colours, and let blast with air hooters. "We tried to make the games exciting," recalled Paul. It was fun. Later, Paul would spend nine years playing football for the club, from junior level through to the senior side. With his subsequent success in Europe and his captaincy of the Australian national team, he is unquestionably and rightly a local hero.

Okon mentioned something else when I asked him about the personal impact of the Stewart Report. It was this: "Maybe my transfer was used as a way to get at other people. That doesn't really concern me so long as at the end something positive came out of it. Maybe it is unfortunate that the only way that some people could get a personal battle going was with my transfer."

The 'personal battle' Okon referred to was between Tony Labbozzetta, former president of Club Marconi, board member of Soccer Australia and eventually its Chairman, and Vince Morizzi, a shopping centre developer, ex-member of Club Marconi, and one-time secretary of the club's football team. The 'battle' would also rope in Remo Nogarotto, a former Marconi official who later launched the Northern Spirit NSL team, was also briefly Chairman of Soccer Australia, and who was elected to the board of Football Federation Australia in 2018. It is a 'personal battle' that could easily be dismissed as an inconsequential suburban spat between local identities but it is also a 'personal battle' that explains the inner workings of Australian soccer in the 1990s and some of the actions of the so-called powerbrokers who were responsible for the position the sport found itself in at the time.

Like the Okons, Vince Morizzi has been involved with Marconi and its soccer teams for many years. When he was young, Morizzi would spend Saturdays cutting the grass on the main pitch and marking out the white lines. During the mid-1960's he even played for the club, albeit with modest talent. Morizzi's brother Joe had sat on Marconi's soccer club committee when it was still an amateur operation and was the soccer club's first-ever president. This was a time, according to Morizzi, when "the people supporting Marconi did it for love. It was total dedication. There was no limelight or any name in the paper. They did it for the love of the game."

In 1977, the National Soccer League, Australia's first national football competition of any code, was inaugurated. Marconi was invited to be one of the foundation clubs (originally on the proviso that the club adopt a less 'ethnic' name). That year, Tony Labbozzetta was president of Marconi's soccer club. Vince Morizzi was club secretary. It placed Morizzi in a position to see exactly what went on within the club. "Not only as far as the soccer was concerned but also as far as everything else," explains Morizzi. In later years, although no longer secretary of the soccer club, Morizzi says he was always in the club's loop. He would have access to the team's dressing room and at one point even led a Marconi team on a tour of Czechoslovakia.

Morizzi recalls first meeting Labbozzetta sometime around 1970. They became good friends, so close that Morizzi says Labbozzetta shed tears in his presence. Morizzi has many stories from the days he used to knock about with Labbozzetta. Some he is prepared to tell, others, he is not. One thing is for sure: Labbozzetta always liked to be his own man. According to Morizzi, Tony would often say that in life, "there were born leaders, people the rest were meant to follow". Labbozzetta was apparently a leader. Morizzi would always be sure to reply: "Let someone else tell you that."

Several years after entering the NSL, Marconi's social club, apparently on the recommendation of Labbozzetta, took over the running of the soccer club. Previously, the two organisations had been separate entities; now they were one. Club Marconi is a registered licensed club and therefore must follow a strict set of government regulations and guidelines, as set down by the NSW Director of Liquor and Gaming. These regulations mean that Marconi's soccer club cannot be managed in the same way as, say, Perth Glory, which is privately owned. On the football field, this is neither here nor there. However, it was a situation that would complicate matters off-field for Labbozzetta.

Labbozzetta was elected president of Club Marconi's social club in 1986. On taking up his new position he now sat at the top of one of Sydney's most lucrative licensed clubs. He had come a long way from his days as a real estate agent and furniture salesman. As he grew into his new role, he surrounded himself with people who were, according to Morizzi, "loyal and true and would not challenge his position or authority".

In 1993, Morizzi and Labbozzetta fell out. Big time. The origins of the dispute were apparently sparked by Morizzi's brother questioning Labbozzetta over details about a proposed building development at the club. Joe Morizzi became frustrated by what he saw as Labbozzetta's evasiveness and took his questions to the club's board. When Vince Morizzi stood up for his brother, the relationship between the close friends chilled. Soon afterwards, a dispute erupted over the lease of a private box at Marconi's soccer ground. Morizzi says that overnight he went from being an exemplary member of the club to an outcast. He claims his membership of Club Marconi was suspended.

In September 1993, Remo Nogarotto, took on Labbozzetta in an election for Club Marconi's presidency. Nogarotto had been on the board of the Marconi licensed club since 1984 and became chairman of its football club in 1989. In the 1993 elections, Nogarotto was hammered in the vote and his position became untenable (to hold office on Marconi's soccer committee it was necessary to be an elected board member). Nogarotto jumped ship and eventually launched his own club, Northern Spirit (a story worth its own book).

During Justice Stewart's investigation of Club Marconi, Nogarotto was called as a key witness. Nogarotto had been at Club Marconi during a crucial period of the club's and Labbozzetta's recent history. Stewart considered that Nogarotto might provide valuable insights. However, Nogarotto suggested Justice Stewart interview Vince Morizzi. Nogarotto explained to Stewart: "If you want to know the ins and outs of the National Soccer League, the start of it, who the players are, where everything is, Vince Morizzi is the guy who knows." Given that Morizzi and Labbozzetta had a falling out after Justice Stewart's investigation, this put Morizzi in an interesting position.

In his report, Donald Stewart described the system of power and patronage that characterised the administration of soccer in Australia as a "complex network of almost Byzantine proportions... especially in the individual soccer clubs". Nothing was black and white. Alongside then-national coach Eddie Thomson, Tony Labbozzetta was the undisputed 'star' of the Stewart Report. Labbozzetta was investigated by Stewart over the methods he employed to transfer Paul Okon from Club Marconi to Club Brugge in Belgium. The major issue concerned a financial discrepancy between the amount of Okon's transfer and the amount that was ultimately deposited into Marconi's bank account. Club Marconi banked $240,000 from Club Brugge for Okon, yet Club Brugge officially paid Club Marconi $515,000. It remains a mystery what happened to the missing money. This is even before we mention the transfer being paid for in cash, and before we mention the lackadaisical attitude of Marconi to its financial record-keeping.

Labbozzetta's account of the transfer was met with scorn by Stewart. "Unfortunately, Mr Labbozzetta obfuscated and prevaricated and his account of what occurred cannot be taken seriously," he wrote. When interviewed by Stewart, Labbozzetta suggested that he was at arm's length in negotiations for the transfer. However, documentation concerning the transfer sets out that Labbozzetta was Club Marconi's representative in negotiations between the two clubs and the player agents. Marconi's own board even empowered Labbozzetta to carry out negotiations on the club's behalf. Labbozzetta told fellow committee members that he alone would be the person to handle Okon's transfer, despite this role rightly being the responsibility of others.

During the inquiry, Stewart told how he had received information that Labbozzetta had berated Australian Soccer Federation chief executive Ian Holmes because he feared Holmes was "undermining" him. The Marconi president, who was also an ASF commissioner, was 'ropeable'. Stewart asked Labbozzetta if he had said to Holmes, "There will certainly be no bloody public statements by the ASF. There are skeletons in the closet and I will expose everyone. Everyone is too busy protecting their arse". Labbozzetta replied to Stewart, "I may have said even worse than that. To be honest, I don't recall."

Labbozzetta also described to Stewart how he felt he was the victim of a conspiracy - not one contrived by Vince Morizzi - "[Morizzi] is insignificant in everything," Labbozzetta has said - but instead one orchestrated by Remo Nogarotto. Dismissing such an allegation, Stewart found there was not a shred of evidence of any conspiracy. At the time, the Marconi president was under pressure and feeling the heat, and not just from Justice Stewart. Concurrent with the Stewart Report, Club Marconi was hauled over the coals by the NSW Liquor Administration Board. The Licensing Court found fifty-eight matters of complaint of which eighteen were found to have breached the law.

"Due to the complexity of the system and the lack of documentation, I was unable to establish an audit trail," said LAB investigator Lois Levi of Marconi's accounting. The club was fined $15,000 and club President Labbozzetta, along with vice-presidents Frank Fontana and Frank Baroni, found themselves having to 'show cause' why they should not be barred from holding office with a NSW licensed club. In 1997, Labbozzetta was found ineligible for office at Club Marconi or any other registered club for a period of two years. Labbozzetta appealed to the NSW Supreme Court, an appeal which was dismissed in 1998. He then appealed again against the severity of the sentence.

"From his own statements, all transfers at Club Marconi came under his control," said Vince Morizzi of the mystery of the Paul Okon transfer. "There is no doubt from the documentation that he was in charge, from the correspondence from Club Brugge to Club Marconi. The club's board then authorised that Labbozzetta was in charge. He was authorised by a motion that he was to handle that particular transfer....it was all with the full knowledge of Tony Labbozzetta."

It must be pointed out, however, that no one has formally proved any wrongdoing on Labbozzetta's part. He frequently defended his position for this reason. As well as a Senate inquiry prompted by Stewart's findings, several high-level police investigations met dead ends. An investigation headed by Superintendent Bob Lysaught, the former head of the Fraud Enforcement Agency, was suspended after Lysaught returned from a $10,000 trip to Belgium claiming that no one at Club Brugge would speak to him. Then Assistant Commissioner Clive Small launched a NSW Police investigation into the affair.

Tony Labbozzetta had heard through the grapevine I was interested in discussing the administration of soccer in Australia. He knew I was intrigued by his relationship with Vince Morizzi, and he knew that I had spoken to Soccer Australia chairman Basil Scarsella about these matters because Scarsella himself had told him.

"I don't have any feuds with anybody," explained Labbozzetta when I asked him if he could shed some light on his relationship with Morizzi, something that had apparently been a factor in his appearance before the Stewart Inquiry and the NSW Licensing Court. "I just do what I think is best for the role that I play. In particular with Club Marconi, it was not I who made the decisions it was the board of the club. In all of the matters that were relevant or irrelevant, Tony Labbozzetta was merely the president."

I asked Labbozzetta if it was true that he and Morizzi had once been good friends but were now estranged. "Maybe, yes, that could be right," he said. "That is not an issue. It is bigger than that. It is bigger than a feud between just one person or another." Labbozzetta explained that Club Marconi had been in a position where it had had to defend breaches of the NSW Licensing Act in court and alleged that several the breaches were "predominantly instigated by a number of people", being not just Vince Morizzi, but his brother Joe, and Nogarotto.

I explained to Labbozzetta that Paul Okon had made a comment to me about a "personal battle" between him and Vince Morizzi. It seemed to have a significant bearing on certain issues.

'Well, Paul Okon is not involved, is he?" Labbozzetta replied. "If Paul Okon wants to bring it up I think he should be very careful and cautious about what he says. If he has not been involved, then I don't think it would be proper of him to make any such suggestions, don't you think?"

"Why would that be?" I asked.

"Why should I tell you about a 'feud' between George Negus and David Hill, for example?" said Labbozzetta, bizarrely raising the names of the former commissioner and the former chairman of Soccer Australia.

"I have nothing to say other than what I have just said to you," said Labbozzetta. "I am no longer the president of Club Marconi, and for me to speak on any issues [regarding] the club is not proper. If you are telling me that Paul Okon has disclosed certain information about Vince Morizzi then that is Paul's view and perhaps you should take it up with Vince Morizzi. I have nothing personal against anyone and nor did I have anything personal against anyone [in the past]. I acted in my capacity as president together with my board of directors and acted in a proper fashion."

Tony Labbozzetta's position in the game was turned on its head when David Hill entered the arena in 1995. Hill, a man with a reputation as a head kicking Mr Fixit, was charged with clearing the deadwood from the Australian soccer scene. Labbozzetta became embarrassed by Hill's approach to reform, as he had originally lobbied for Hill's election as chairman of Soccer Australia. NSL clubs Heidelberg United, Parramatta Eagles and Brunswick Juventus were expelled from the league, a no-compromise move that signalled to Labbozzetta that no one was safe from Hill's axe. As Marconi's representative to the NSL, Labbozzetta had many opportunities to clash with Hill.

Labbozzetta made headlines when he opposed Hill's demand that 'ethnic' emblems be banished from what today would be called an NSL club's 'brand'. A problem was that Labbozzetta's argument that Marconi's Italian heritage was always part of the club and was included in the club's original badge fell apart when a club blazer from 1958 was presented to David Hill proving otherwise. Joe Morizzi, a founding Marconi member who provided the blazer to Hill, was subsequently suspended from the club.

"David Hill was right about everything," recalls Nick Tana, founder of Perth Glory, which became Australia's best-supported soccer club when it entered the league in 1996. "He got derailed when it became a 'Tony and David Show'. We would all attend a meeting and it would be a confrontation between David and Tony. It became farcical."

Labbozzetta railed against Hill's appointment of Terry Venables as national coach, complained about continual litigation from those parties disgruntled by Hill's hard-nosed decisions, and criticised the expense of the 1998 World Cup qualifying campaign. This was despite the expenses being authorised by a committee chaired by Basil Scarsella, who eventually replace Hill as Soccer Australia chairman. Labbozzetta also attempted to influence public opinion. In early 1998 he visited the offices of Australian and British Soccer Weekly, a must-read soccer news magazine of the time. Labbozzetta lobbied the magazine to publish a negative article about Hill which eventually saw then-editor Micky Brock win an Industrial Relations Commission case for unfair dismissal when he refused to comply with the publisher's order to print the story.

The Labbozzetta-Hill feud hit me head-on in 1998. I interviewed Hill for the July 1998 edition of Playboy magazine in which he took a deep dive on his tenure as chairman of Soccer Australia. He talked about Australia's World Cup play-off with Iran, Terry Venables, the NSL, and his own interest in running for political office. Legend has it that the most unlikely people were buying up copies of the magazine in bulk from newsagents in western Sydney and the reason for the spike in sales was not a photo spread with a famous classical violinist nor my interview with Tim Rogers of the band You Am I. What perked interest in the magazine was an answer Hill gave to one particular question.

Asked about the future for some clubs in the National Soccer League, Hill cited Marconi as an example of a club that "isn't even representative of the south-west of Sydney. It's a facility for the members of the Marconi Social Club ... the football club is a financial disaster." So far so good, but the following quote is where it got interesting. Hill referenced the club transferring a player and where the transfer fee ended up. The quote sparked legal action from Club Marconi – but not Labbozzetta. The legal claim was that the quote disparaged all Club Marconi members. There was only one catch. My notes suggested Hill hadn't said the quote as printed and neither had the story as I submitted it.

I was flown back from Europe where I'd just wrapped up covering the 1998 World Cup to find the tape recording of the interview. I got off the plane at Sydney airport and took a cab to a house in the eastern suburbs where the tape was in one of 100 storage boxes. In a run of luck perhaps not seen since, the tape was in the first box opened (I'm not kidding about the 100 boxes) and revealed that my recollection of what Hill had said was accurate. It turned out an over-zealous sub-editor at the magazine had changed one word that altered the interpretation of where the hypothetical transfer fee had ended up. The claim was settled and never reached the courts.

Hill resigned his Soccer Australia chairmanship to unsuccessfully contest a seat in the October 1998 federal election. Within months, Labbozzetta had navigated his return to Soccer Australia and in doing so defeated Nick Tana in an election to be the NSL's representative on the board. Clubs sided along predictable lines. Those in favour of the status quo voted for Labbozzetta: old school clubs Sydney United, South Melbourne, Marconi, Adelaide City, West Adelaide, Melbourne Knights and Gippsland. Those in favour of reform were for Tana: Perth Glory, Carlton, Northern Spirit, Sydney Olympic, Wollongong Wolves, Canberra Cosmos and Brisbane Strikers. Labbozzetta won by one vote when Newcastle Breakers, perhaps surprisingly, sided with him.

"He came in for a scare," grins Tana. "It was awfully close. Tony called me up twice and asked me to call it off. He told me what his agenda was and clearly, as far as I was concerned, he was out of line. His was not my agenda."

In 1993, Nick Tana turned up to watch Australia play New Zealand at Olympic Park in Melbourne. Besides an interest in Australia's World Cup progress, the fast-food millionaire was in town to raise support for the not unreasonable idea of a Perth team joining the NSL. A small oversight from Australian soccer's would-be powerbrokers had denied a Western Australian team a place in the national league since its inception sixteen years earlier.

Tana was sitting next to Sam Papasavas, an influential Soccer Australia commissioner and then-chairman of the NSL. Papasavas turned to Tana and smugly said, "What possible benefit can a Perth team bring to us?" Tana was taken aback at the remark. Papasavas died soon after and never saw Perch Glory and its fervent supporters revolutionise soccer in Australia. "We just chipped away," muses Tana. "At the end of the day sanity prevailed."

Papasavas's attitude was not uncommon. In 1961, Channel Seven in Melbourne was searching for a sport to broadcast on winter Saturday afternoons. The Victorian Football League felt live TV coverage would adversely affect its Aussie Rules match attendances, so Channel Seven arranged a meeting with the Australian Soccer Federation to negotiate the broadcast rights for live soccer fixtures.

The powerful Herald and Weekly Times newspaper group secretly signalled that it would throw its promotional weight behind soccer if Seven secured the deal. The ASF couldn't believe its luck. Its executive committee put the news to its members, but inexplicably the proposal was rejected on the grounds that there was a Greek conspiracy: according to some parties, Theo Marmaras, the then-ASF chief, had clearly cut a deal for the Greek clubs at the expense of the non-Greeks. No soccer on TV. The following year, the VFL realised its mistake and joined forces with Channel Seven.

In 1994 Donald Stewart opened his report to the ASF with a dramatic quote from Shakespeare's *The Tempest*:

Full fathom five thy father lies, Of his bones are coral made;

Those are pearls that made his eyes:

 Nothing of him that doth fade,

But doth suffer a sea-change

Into something rich and strange.

Sea-nymphs hourly ring his knell:

Ding-dong.

Hark! Now I hear them, - ding-dong, bell.

Stewart famously stated that "nothing less than a sea change would satisfy the critics of the administration of soccer in Australia". Yet the more things changed the more things stayed the same.

As Remo Nogarotto told me, "My single greatest disappointment [from] the Stewart Report and the period that flowed from it [is that] the sort of sea change that I would have liked, which would have swept away individuals as well as practices, hasn't really happened. There are still people there [in Australian soccer] who are clinging to all sorts of vestiges of power. From that perspective I am a little disappointed."

When Nogarotto established Northern Spirit he encountered similar obstacles to Nick Tana in Perth, except Nogarotto received death threats for his trouble. "Both myself and my family were subjected to threatening phone calls," he says. 'I certainly received a lot more when I was giving evidence for the Stewart Report. That was not a pleasant time in my life."

Why would people would go to such lengths. "I don't know," he said. "I am staggered. [It was] a football club."

Labbozzetta's legal team sought to reopen the findings of fact made by Justice Keating in 1997. The Full Bench found that the grounds proved were considered 'established. The March 2000 finding considered that Labbozzetta was not in breach on three instances. One occasion, in March 1993, Labbozzetta was reimbursed by Club Marconi for $700 of expenses when he took Sepp Blatter, then General Secretary of FIFA, and other FIFA officials to lunch in East Sydney. In September of the same year, Labbozzetta was reimbursed for $270 expenses when he paid for a lunch entertaining the president of Italian club Reggina. Labbozzetta said in his defence that the meetings proved fruitful in the ultimate transfer of Steve Corica from Club Marconi to Leicester City. The Full Bench found that Labbozzetta's actions on these occasions did not warrant any action against him.

However, it was found that Labbozzetta was involved in breaches involving cash advances from Club Marconi, cash advances using his American Express card, expenses relating to his 25rh wedding anniversary, and the failure to keep correct accounts and books in respect of the Paul Okon transfer to Club Brugge. But it was also decided that Labbozzetta's credibility could not be questioned based on evidence he gave in court. The Licensing Court, having praised Labbozzetta for his contributions to Club Marconi and charitable organisations, judged that having effectively "served nine months for these breaches, no further disciplinary action was warranted".

In what can only be described as a pioneering masterstroke of fake news decades prior to that term becoming mainstream, Labbozzetta issued a media release under the headline "Soccer Chief Cleared", which claimed that 'the book has finally been closed on one of Australian soccer's greatest controversies". Labbozzetta claimed that he had been "vindicated". Les Murray, hosting SBS-TVs flagship World Sport news program, breathlessly reported Labbozzetta's claim unchallenged, as did the front page of the March 21 edition of Australian and British Soccer Weekly, which published the Labbozzetta-issued press release and selected contents of the finding. I called the editor of ABSW to ask who the source of the front-page lead story was. He said it had come from the horse's mouth. He had not read the finding himself.

In February 2001, Labbozzetta was elected chairman of Soccer Australia. It was an era marked by administrative staff bizarrely standing to attention when he visited the organization's head office in central Sydney, Trumpian lies coming out of the same office about the structure of some of the federation's business deals, and police calling me to ask where I'd got information from while reporting on Marconi and Soccer Australia business. To be fair, this was the same police force whose members would meet me in western Sydney and - no touching! - show me their work in investigating people and business connected to Australian soccer. The results from some of this reporting was being read in Canberra and would eventually help convince the federal government the sport's administration needed an overhaul.

Around the same time, on a sunny Saturday afternoon, a meeting took place at a house in the Sydney suburbs. The reason for the meeting was to address the public attention certain people from the community were receiving. It was not how things should be done, it was explained. The public attention was a byproduct of a feud between two camps in Sydney. A man flew to Sydney from Italy to deliver the firm message to everyone in attendance: "This all has to stop." I received text messages describing the event as it had played out: the Italian visitor at the head of a horseshoe table, the formality of the occasion, the shots of alcohol being offered to everyone at the table, the views from both sides in attendance, the silence, the nodding, the ultimatums. "It was like a scene out of a movie," read one text.

The movie, though, was real life and the movie was Australian soccer in the 1990s and early 2000s. A few years later, in 2003, Tony Labbozzetta was no longer Soccer Australia chairman and not getting so much attention. The NSL was shut down and Marconi was no longer a big deal. Soccer Australia was in the bin. Billionaire Frank Lowy stepped up and into the vacuum. Which is a whole other story.

FRANK FARINA: "THAT'S NOT A BULLSHIT ANSWER."

Sydney, September 2001

It was believed that November, 2001, would make or break Frank Farina. He'd just steered Australia to a 1-0 win over France at the Confederations Cup and a 31-0 win over American Samoa in a World Cup qualifier but the real business was to be a play-off against CONMEBOL's fifth-placed team - Uruguay. "By the end of the month, Farina will be either a dead-set legend or he'll join the now-long list of Australian World Cup duds," I wrote.

I was wrong that November would make or break him (that would take a little longer) and Farina proved you could be both a dead-set legend and World Cup dud at the same time. He held on to his job - precariously - for almost four more years. This interview, which took place before the Uruguay play-off, was originally published in *FHM* magazine (RIP). Farina was playful but also played hard.

You were born in Darwin and grew up in Papua New Guinea. Can you wrestle a crocodile?

There is a photo of me and some mates taken at the Kokoda Trail Motel in Port Moresby with a sign saying "No Swimming. Crocodiles. Big 'Uns". We'd still go swimming, though. We used to think that if the water was up to our waists then we were OK. How stupid were we?

One of your nicknames if Fingerbone. Please explain.

That was from my first passport photo when we went on trips with the Australian youth team. One of the boys reckoned I Looked Like David Gulpilil out of Storm Boy.

You once shared a flat with Robbie Slater, right?

No, not quite. His then-girlfriend shared my two-bedroom apartment. But Robbie still owes me from when he head-butted a wall. It was the night before we went to the Olympics [in 1988].

There are photos to back it up. He had this big red gravel rash on his forehead. He told everyone that he fell over. I've never told anyone the truth. I've kept it a secret for this long. I must send him the bill.

Hang on - didn't you and Slater have a big bust up at training with the Socceroos in 1993?

We had a bit of a blue but I think it was more like handbags at 10 paces.

Could you take him today?

Haha. I don't think me and Robbie will ever be fighters, put it that way.

You played for Brugge for several years. They call that place the "City Of 1,000 Beers"...

... And I drank at least 999 of them.

Not all of them, then?

No. Always leave a little bit.

You were one of the first Australians to head overseas and be successful in Europe. These days it seems that anyone who can kick a ball is giving it a go. Is that good or bad?

It's a catch-22 situation. It is beneficial for our national team... but it's also weakening our domestic competition. There's not a lot we can do about it. You can't stop the players from wanting to go overseas.

Do you think people in Australia realise what our soccer players have achieved overseas?

No. Even some football people don't really understand. They don't know about how you have to change your lifestyle and live without family and friends. They don't realise what these guys go through to get where they are. Harry Kewell left for England at the age of 15. People criticise some of the things that he does but he's gone through a lot to be successful.

Do you wish that you'd played more in England?

When I was in Europe, Italy was regarded as the biggest and

best league. You never saw Italians or Frenchmen wanting to go to England. I was briefly at Sheffield Wednesday at the same time as Eric Cantona. I was talking to their manager Trevor Francis and he said he thought Cantona was a bit of a fanny merchant and he'd struggle in England, haha.

Are Italian crowds the craziest?

They're certainly among the most passionate. I played at Bari, which is down in the south and a poor area of Italy. Football was an important thing that they'd look forward to during the week. When we were winning we were like gods and when we lost they wouldn't even look at us.

What's the wildest crowd you've played in front of?

The World Youth Cup in 1983 against Mexico at the Azteca Stadium in Mexico City. That was in front of 110,000 people. I remember warming up and it was like a beehive. When they scored the place exploded. It was like a bomb. Then we scored and there was complete silence.

Which international team has the worst attitude?

In my experience, I would say that it's Israel They could dish it out but they could never take it. If you look at teams like Brazil and France, they are difficult to play against because they're technically brilliant and physically strong.

Who was better: Pete, Maradona, or Johan Cruyff?

It's very hard to judge but I'd have to say Pele. He scored over 1,000 goals and won three World Cups and I don't think that will ever be repeated.

Who are the best three players today?

I'd have to say Marcel Desailly [Chelsea and France], Zinedine Zidane [Réal Madrid and France], and Luis Ago [Réal Madrid and Portugal].

Will an Australian ever be in that top three?

Oh, yeah. Definitely, with the likes of Kewell and Viduka. Don't forget that Harry is only 22 and Mark is 25. When you have clubs Like Réal Madrid and AC Milan chasing those guys then we're not that far of. Maybe we have to be on the world stage for one of our players to receive that accolade and qualifying for the World Cup will pit us against the best in the world.

How come Australia hasn't qualified for the World Cup since 1974?

Over the past 27 years it's always come down to just two games. If you put any country in the world into that situation - a play-off - they'd struggle every time. Your best players can be injured or unavailable and it all comes down to that two-week period. It's completely unfair. Having said that, in the past we just weren't good enough to get over the line. We could talk about Argentina in 1993. We had a 1-1 result at home against them and everyone was going on about how good it was. In 1997, we were very unlucky. Anyone who says you don't need luck doesn't understand football.

Do you get sick to death of talking about the World Cup qualifier?

No. It just shows how important it is for our county. One of the most important things for soccer in Australia is that we must push for direct qualification for Oceania. Whether that takes blackmail, bribery, sucking up, whatever you want to call it, then we have to do it. That will change Australian soccer not only at international level but also at the national and grassroots level. If we know that every four years Australia is going to be at the biggest event in the world then everything changes.

If you could coach any team in the world, who would you take?

I'm in charge of that team at the moment. The first Australian side to qualify for the World Cup since 74. And that's not a bullshit answer.

NICKY SALAPU CAN COUNT TO 57

Coffs Harbour, April 2001

Nicky Salapu picked the ball from his net 57 times during his country's four World Cup qualifiers over Easter, but then he is the goalkeeper for American Samoa, officially the worst national team in the world.

For Oceania's qualifying competition for the 2002 World Cup, Group One was a mini-tournament of inglorious world records. Held in Coffs Harbour, a vacation resort on the northern New South Wales coast, the games were hard work for most of the competing nations. Ironically for Australia, the tournament was a holiday at home.

Australia's Archie Thompson scored 13 of the record 31 goals the Socceroos racked up against American Samoa, a score line that broke the Socceroos' own record for a tournament set one game earlier by beating Tonga 22-0. Australia topped their group with a goal difference of plus-66. The scores made headlines around the world. Thompson became an international star for 24 hours while coaches, officials, and the media ridiculed Oceania's credibility with a gusto not seen since Oceania Football Confederation president Charlie Dempsey handed Germany the 2006 World Cup.

Two nights after shot after shot whistled past his ears, I sat with Salapu in his motel room to watch Leeds United beat Liverpool on Australian cable TV. European football was rare on American Samoan television - airtime dominated by US sports from broadcasters like ESPN.

"I like Michael Owen," Salapu said, pointing to the small screen in the corner of his room and bearing no grudges against strikers. In every way, the Premier League is a million miles from the rocky grounds and village teams the internationals of American Samoa are familiar with. Salapu, 20-years-old, recognised Harry Kewell on the screen and said it was funny an outfield player would sometimes wear woolen gloves, just like a goalkeeper.

He stopped laughing when it was pointed out Kewell is Australian. Club versus country wrangles meant Kewell had missed the Coffs Harbor tournament but could have lined up against Salapu a few days earlier. There was silence in the room before teammate Avele Mauga offered his view.

"I think it's OK for Kewell to play against Liverpool rather than us, then," he said a with a smile. "Australia were already so fast the other night it seemed they were riding motorbikes."

Hot takes to results during these group games suggested Oceania, and its World Cup qualifying process, are little more than a farce. Some critics went so far as to say the confederation should be shut down and merged with Asia. It's not a terrible idea. Rangers manager Dick Advocaat and Coventry City's Gordon Strachan moaned about their players called into Australia's squad: why should these players be dragged across the other side of the world for "Mickey Mouse" qualifiers? The world game? The world stops at the bottom of Britain, apparently.

The eternal (and increasingly tedious) club versus country debate took another twist during Australia's preparation for these matches. Soccer Australia, hoping to avoid fixture congestion in June when Australia would take part in the Confederations Cup and World Cup qualifiers, made a controversial deal with FIFA to the effect that no Europe-based players would be called up for the April tournament against the will of their clubs. The result: Mark Viduka, Kewell, Paul Okon, Mark Schwarzer and Danny Tiatto stayed in Britain, while Craig Moore and Tony Vidmar of Rangers, John Aloisi of Coventry, Kevin Muscat of Wolves and West Ham's Hayden Foxe caught the plane to Australia. In what could prove an interesting precedent, the clubs effectively called the selection shots. Advocaat and Strachan would have saved hot air had they paid attention to the agreement, no matter how ad hoc.

Not that the Australian players could be blamed for surrendering the dog end of a British winter for an Easter vacation. The World Cup games were played at Coffs Harbour, seven hours' drive north of Sydney (the town's total taxis: 17). Australia's HQ was a secluded five-star resort with manicured lawns, its own golf course, and room rates peaking at US$1,500 - although the Australian team received attractive discounts. American Samoa were three to a room at a $100-a-night highway motel. There were other differences. American Samoa's players received $100 for the entire tournament. The Australians picked up $300 a day with each squad member scoring $2,000 for each win.

Fiji's participation was also touch-and-go. The Australian government briefly lifted sporting sanctions in place since the 2000 coup d'état that allowed the team to travel to Australia. Fiji responded by battling to a creditable 2-0 loss against their hosts. Fiji's players were theoretically playing for a $5,000 bonus, although to get it they not only had to beat Australia but actually qualify for the 2002 finals. Inspiration at training sessions was helped by a barrel of kava, a traditional blow-your-mind anesthetic drink, available for players and officials on the sidelines.

Fiji coach Billy Singh warmed up the tournament with a war of words with Frank Farina after the Australia coach warned his players to beware of Fiji tactics that might include "biting and scratching". In the event, Singh didn't employ such a roughhouse strategy but did restore pride to the island nations in the tournament's "crunch" game. Had Fiji striker Josaia Sauturaga, a junior with Sydney club Marconi, not fluffed an open goal at 1-0 right on half-time, the result might even have been a little different. "We proved everyone wrong," said Fiji's Australian-based striker Esala Masi after the match. "We can keep our cool. We can play."

Oceania could be a benchmark for the development of football as a true world sport. In 20 years' time, it's just possible Australia won't be the only Oceania side to have beaten Scotland 2-0 at Hampden Park. American Samoa may be last on FIFA's rankings, and probably won't be the team to humble a European side, but it's the only country in the world where football is a part of the official national education program. American Samoa joined FIFA in 1998 and the national association has since successfully campaigned to have the sport take a compulsory place, for boys and girls, alongside maths and history in schools.

Back in his motel room, watching Leeds play Liverpool, Nicky Salapu whistled when he heard of the riches available to Premiership players. For his team, and perhaps much of Oceania, money is attractive but not what football is necessarily about. "We had to admire American Samoa," said one Australian defender. "They knew they were going to be pumped but they still lined up with two guys up front. They were going to have a go."

American Samoa's only shot that night, a lame trickle from just over the halfway line, received the biggest cheer of the game. But they stuck with twin strikers until the final whistle. Salapu and several teammates had missed a string of matches for their clubs back home. There was no struggle to get away. "The clubs were happy because we're away representing our country," Salapu explained. Gordon Strachan and Dick Advocaat need not attempt to understand just what that means.

Critics of the current qualifying system would like to see giant versus minnow mismatches abandoned and smaller nations form an Oceania second division. Players and officials from the condemned countries appear united: they don't want it. The night after the loss to Australia, at the Saturday night buffet dinner at the Coffs Harbour RSL club, the squad held hands and prayed before eating. As they eventually ate, the American Samoans talked about looking forward to their next potential meeting with Australia. They predicted possible scores: 25-0? 20-0? 15-0? It wouldn't matter, according to the worst team in the world.

They were up for it.

It's the World Cup.

A CAULDRON OF HELL WITH A BOTTLE OF WINE

Montevideo, November 2001

Three strikes and you're out, and a triple lash from Uruguay in Montevideo sent Australia crashing out of the World Cup without qualifying for the finals for the seventh time in succession. The first and last time the Socceroos made it to the finals was in 1974. On the past five occasions, Australia was eliminated in what were effectively sudden death play-offs: against Scotland, Israel, Argentina, Iran and now Uruguay. Conspiracy theories, administrative blunders, plain bad luck and the comeback of Diego Maradona have all contributed to past failures.

This time, however, there can be no complaints. Australia were beaten fair and square. Although most of the team played in Europe, the entire expedition appeared riddled with inexperience and naivety. Australia lost to a team that was confident and had no doubt about its destiny. Uruguay's team bus got stuck as it attempted to negotiate the driveway into Montevideo's Estadio Centenario but that was almost the only thing that went wrong for the South Americans.

"I honestly thought we would score in Uruguay," said coach Frank Farina after the match. "We had a few good chances but we didn't take them. We needed to score and we didn't. We just didn't have it."

You can say that again, Frankie. The result mirrored the football landscape back in Australia. Soccer Australia, the governing body, is a financial disaster. It was anticipating the $6 million guaranteed from qualification to save it from ruin. After years of financial mismanagement that verged on corruption, a new administration elected in August 2001 is now in danger of collapse. There is simply no money.

The National Soccer League lurches from crisis to crisis with fewer than a handful of teams of interest to the general public. Had

Australia qualified, a plan was in place to shut down the league and relaunch it with a set-up styled on America's Major League Soccer. It may even have worked. Now we will probably never know.

After the final whistle in Montevideo, travelling from the stadium to the city centre by taxi was almost impossible. Montevideo's main roads were clogged to standstill as the fans sang ¡Soy Celeste! (I am sky blue), the catchy Uruguay theme song. The result may have been a sure thing but in Montevideo they liked to celebrate.

"Uruguay's economy is stuffed and the people have little money, so qualifying for the World Cup is a massive boost for the people and the country as a whole," said the taxi driver, with one hand firmly pressed to his car's horn.

Several of Australia's apparent stars, almost all of whom play in the Premiership, Championship, or Scottish Premier League, failed to stand up and make themselves count in Australian soccer's hour and a half of need. Brett Emerton of Feyenoord, long touted as the next big thing, showed he has a way to grow yet. Captain Paul Okon of Middlesbrough, loved by Terry Venables but less so by Steve McClaren, was crowded out of the game by sky blue shirts.

The decision to play Harry Kewell as a striker backfired badly. Mark Viduka had no service and no one to play off. 1860 Munich's Paul Agostino, who created many problems for Uruguay when he came on as a second-half substitute in the first leg in Melbourne, wasn't introduced in Montevideo until late in the game. Australia's best periods were with two strikers and Kewell wide on the left. The talk back at the media hotel was that that egos rather than common sense helped pick the team, up front at least. While it was 2-0 until the 90th minute and an Australian goal would have sent the Socceroos through that never looked - nor felt - like happening.

Farina's immediate future is now in doubt. Before the second leg, Soccer Australia's deputy chairman Greg Woods came out in support of him being offered a new contract, but the Woods view is not necessarily shared by other Soccer Australia board members. After a run of impressive results (if not always fluent performances) this year, Farina has been subject to continual rumours linking him with lucrative coaching jobs in Japan and some smaller clubs in Europe.

However, despite beating Scotland in 2000, France and Brazil at the Confederations Cup in June, and earning a deserved 1-1 draw against France in a friendly before the World Cup play-off, Uruguay's 3-0 win was emphatic. It was Australia's most convincing defeat in World Cup games since the 1960s. Not since North Korea beat them 6-1 in a play-off in "neutral" Cambodia for a place at the 1966 finals had the Socceroos been so outclassed.

The irony is that this crop of players was supposed to be the Golden Team, graduates of a vibrant youth system that had seen Australia perform impressively at almost every World Youth Cup since 1991. Farina said he had built a team big on spirit. This appears to be true, but spirit alone was not going to be enough to overcome equally inspired, but technically superior, opponents.

"I was asked previously if I would be happy with 1-0 in Melbourne and I said I would settle for that straight away," said Frank Farina after the first leg win in Melbourne. "But there are still 90 minutes to go in an atmosphere which will be hostile if not worse."

Australia was beaten psychologically the minute they stepped off the plane from Australia. A fired-up mob of locals, apparently paid to cause trouble by someone, pushed and shoved the players as they moved from the arrivals hall to the team bus and several members of the delegation and the squad were spat on. TV pictures of the fracas were relayed back to Australia. The Australian tabloid media, always keen to have a good go if xenophobia is involved, beat the hell out of the incident. Animals! and Bloody Disgrace accompanied pictures of midfielder Steve Corica ducking for cover.

The Australian delegation, in its wisdom, went into a Montevideo lock down. A request was made to FIFA to shift the game to a neutral venue (Buenos Aires? Fiji? London?), the players were not allowed to leave the team hotel, and for some unexplained reason non-Australian media were banned from the daily press conferences. This didn't leave Agence France Presse, Associated Press, Reuters, or the man from the BBC with the best impression of Australian hospitality.

To underline how absurd the situation became, even Australia's prime minister, John Howard, a man whose global vision extended to winning an election on an anti-refugee platform and declaring cricketer Sir Donald Bradman the greatest sportsman of all time, stepped in to the mess by declaring the push-and shove equivalent to an international diplomatic incident.

Some Australian media predicted Montevideo would turn into a "cauldron of hell" for the visiting Australians on the day of the game. Much was made of so-called escape plans and high-level security but, in reality, Uruguay and its people rank among the friendliest on the planet.

"Did you expect to win?" asked the waiter at a neighbourhood restaurant after the match. Well, yes and no. He offered a bottle of wine - "From Argentina!" - on the house to dull any pain. Families, young couples, groups of young men, and young children continued celebrations long into the Montevideo night.

It was dark but the streets were filled with children playing with footballs, re-enacting the goals scored by Dario Silva and Richard Morales, now national heroes for Uruguay. Australian kids will have to wait at least another four years before they get to play a similar game. Australians are used to the regular four-year cycles, but this one will seem particularly long.

IN OCEANIA, NO ONE CAN HEAR YOU SCREAM

Paris, June 2003

After FIFA backflipped on Oceania's guaranteed place at the World Cup, neither Sepp Blatter nor UEFA's Lennart Johansson should consider taking holidays in the South Pacific for the next few years. The two Europeans would normally receive excellent hospitality from southern hemisphere hosts, but, as figurehead and architect of FIFA's turnaround on Oceania's direct entry to World Cup finals, those days are gone.

Oceania's (in)significance to the rest of the football world was underlined in the way FIFA broke the news. A June 28 press release trumpeted the 2006 World Cup would be played by 32 teams (so no change) but revealed in a later paragraph that Oceania had lost its direct place while South America had gained another (all change).

The news created barely a ripple in Europe. In Australia, New Zealand, and across the Pacific, it was tidal waves all around. "This is a nightmare," Australia coach Frank Farina said to anyone who would listen. "We should disband Oceania. What's the point of Oceania without a World Cup place? If we are a confederation, we should enjoy the same privileges as the others."

Basil Scarsella, the usually diplomatic Australian president of the Oceania Football Confederation, walked out of the June 28 FIFA meeting in Paris when the vote was passed 22-1. The OFC was the lone dissenter. "It's unethical, it's immoral, call it what you like," he said.

Initially, FIFA suggested administrative chaos in Australia and New Zealand's poor performance at the recent Confederations Cup were to blame. Certainly, Soccer Australia had suffered corporate anarchy in recent times but a government-initiated coup earlier in the year saw Frank Lowy, the country's soccer-loving third-richest man, installed as the sport's apparent saviour.

"To blame us is just a convenient excuse," said Soccer New Zealand chief Bill McGowan. "If you're going to use that argument, then what about Saudi Arabia at the last World Cup? I don't see anyone talking about taking a place off the Asians."

Had Australia qualified directly for the 2001 World Cup as OFC winners, they would not have embarrassed the region. The Socceroos' track record over the 24 months to 2003 had seen victories over France, Brazil, and Mexico at the 2001 Confederations Cup and England at Upton Park. "This is all about politics and nothing about football," McGowan added. "I had a meeting with Blatter and [FIFA chief executive] Urs Linsi in Paris [before the decision] and they didn't mention anything about this at all. It's just bizarre."

The fall-out from the flip saw the return of Charlie Dempsey, the former OFC president whose infamous non-vote handed the 2006 finals to Germany rather than South Africa. Dempsey, now an "honorary advisor" (whatever that is) to OFC, claimed he knew FIFA was set to reverse its decision two days prior to the vote. Unfortunately, he failed to tell any OFC delegates his news.

Both Australia and New Zealand claimed the backflip has jeopardised commercial arrangements that were put in place earlier in the year and one OFC country is now no longer guaranteed the approximate US$6 million that teams earn for qualification - a big boost in the cash-starved region.

It was suggested the decision may have had big implications for Blatter beyond South Pacific holiday plans. Oceania unanimously supported Blatter in his 2002 reelection campaign. After all, his daughter worked for Soccer Australia during the 1990s. Embarrassing scenes took place when Blatter's rival, Issa Hayatou, arrived in the region to put his case for support: few Oceania delegates would listen to the African. Blatter, even with claims he had nothing to do with the decision, will probably not enjoy such blind backing again.

So, what next for Oceania? More of the same, no doubt. Like Mexico with Concacaf during the 1960s, 1970s and 1980s, Australia will continue to dominate the region. For World Cup qualification, the

Socceroos will win games by cricket scores and then face a sudden-death playoff against a desperate, battle-hardened opponent given a second, or even third, life. The latest FIFA slap may encourage OFC to pursue more active ties with Asia and Concacaf and combine qualification campaigns, but that interest is mostly unrequited.

"We empathise with Oceania but the idea of a four-way play-off all comes too late," Concacaf general secretary Chuck Blazer told me. "We have marketing plans and have sold TV rights packages and our members have made plans for their own professional leagues. It is not whether we can accommodate a team from Oceania, it is how we change a system we had in place six months ago."

If anyone would listen, Oceania would argue the exact same thing.

LIKE THEIR PLAYERS, AUSTRALIAN AGENTS TASTE THE BIG TIME

Leeds, July 2003

Harry Kewell's manager Bernie Mandic collected an estimated $6 million from Leeds United by negotiating the Socceroo star's transfer to Liverpool - and earned the wrath of the Yorkshire club and its fans.

Leeds United, acting like a jilted lover, yesterday released correspondence between Mandic and the club to explain how it came to pay the Australian almost 40 percent of the fee it received from Liverpool. Australian agents, however, backed Mandic saying he earned what he deserved for marshalling Kewell's career over the past five years.

"Bernie has done a tremendous job in cashing in for the player and has cashed in for himself," said Lou Sticca, the Melbourne-based agent who negotiated a move to Scottish Premier League side Hearts for ex-South Melbourne defender Patrick Kisnorbo.

"There are those who are critical of Bernie, there are those who are jealous of him, and there are those who will spite him," Sticca said. "I think he has done a terrific job. He has done me a favour because when I now talk to clubs in Europe he has set a benchmark for Australian agents."

Leeds United can claim that the £2 million fee paid to the Croatia-based company with which Mandic works was exorbitant but in the high-flying world of elite football - the ranks of which Harry Kewell is now destined to join - huge fees paid to agents reflect the market value of the players.

Rio Ferdinand moved from Leeds United to Manchester United this time last year in a $90 million deal that would have provided Pini Zahavi, an Israeli agent and friend of United manager Sir Alex Ferguson, around $9 million if he took a basic 10 percent cut of the move.

British agents made up to $3 million from Manchester United when Mark Bosnich moved from Aston Villa to Old Trafford in 1999 on a free transfer. The transfer did not involve United paying Villa a fee because the goalkeeper's contract had expired - a situation Leeds would have found themselves in next year had Harry Kewell opted to not move this season.

Leo Karis, who represents Leeds United's Paul Okon as well as Mark Bosnich, believes Leeds need to balance Mandic's fee with what Kewell earned the club during his nine seasons there.

"If it had not been for Harry Kewell and his team mates then Leeds would be facing an additional $50 million loss this past season," Karis said. "Had Harry and the players not excelled at the end of the season, Leeds would have dropped to the first division and they would have lost television money, sponsorships, gate receipts, and merchandising. That would have been up to $150 million. They need to balance the Mandic fee out."

According to industry insiders the typical agent's commission for a basic Premier League deal is not less than $150,000 - down from several seasons ago where introducing a player to a club could net an agent $300,000.

At the other end of the scale, Alain Migliaccio, a Spanish-based French agent who represents Zinedine Zidane, is understood to have received $12 million for his role in delivering Zidane to Réal Madrid from Juventus two seasons ago.

"We don't know how much Zidane gives him for negotiating his wage at Real so it is possible that maybe he made $20 million off the whole deal," said Alain Barataud, one of 28 Australian agents licensed by FIFA.

"One thing is for sure. He can stop working already if he wants."

Barataud works from his home in Bondi but has spent the past week in Mexico City negotiating a deal for a Uruguayan client with a Mexican club. This weekend, he is in Geneva having negotiated a three-year deal for a Japanese player, Nayoki Imaya, to join Swiss club Neuchatel Xamax from NSW Super League side Blacktown City. Next week Barataud begins negotiations with French sides Bordeaux and Paris-St Germain over a proposed move for Socceroo Scott Chipperfield from FC Basel.

"Only top players can bring you what Harry Kewell has earned Bernie," Barataud said. "When Scott Chipperfield went from Wollongong to Basel, *the agen*t's commission was $200,000, split three ways between three different agents."

Barataud had to involve other agents in Chipperfield's initial move to Basel because, at the time, he was not licensed with FIFA. The practice is common and explains why Mandic, who is not licensed by FIFA, can negotiate big money deals by forging alliances with colleagues, including Italian Giovanni Branchini.

Branchini represents Ronaldo and holds European marketing rights for Harry Kewell, hinting that the superstar Socceroo may be due one more big money move before he hangs up his boots.

"We deal with very small numbers in sport in Australia," said Leo Karis, explaining some of the reaction to Mandic's return.

"I have said this before but Harry Kewell is worth more than the entire National Rugby League and David Beckham is worth more than the NRL, AFL, and ARU combined."

"That's what you get when you have a player, albeit a very talented player, in a global game."

THE INVISIBLE MAN

Madrid, September 2003

If this story was a movie, the opening scene might have Andy Bernal nudging a Range Rover through dark Madrid streets. But crowded as they are on this night, these are not postcard streets – skinny, old, full of bars, restaurants, and tourists. These are the expensive suburban streets of Madrid's privileged rich in La Moraleja, Madrid's own Beverly Hills.

It's September 2003, but the night is still warm in the Spanish capital. The Range Rover Bernal drives edges past parked cars, crowds of onlookers, and flashing paparazzi, their cameras exploding light in the dark. With a nod to security guards standing out the front, carefully scrutinising all arrivals, Bernal swings his car through the front gates of a vast mansion, up a long curving driveway, and comes to a stop in a car park lined with very expensive sports cars.

Bernal jumps from the Range Rover and guides his companion toward a side gate that leads around a vast house and into a back garden the size of several football fields. They hear the music – loud, brash, fun, Latin – before the scene fully reveals itself. And what a scene: a thumping Mardi Gras of bands, music, dancing, food, drink. It's like Rio De Janeiro - except in Madrid. This is something quite unlike anything Bernal had ever before witnessed.

"Welcome to... Madrid," he laughs, smiling at his companion.

David Beckham – for it was the superstar soccer player was at Bernal's side that night – nodded and he too smiled. This occasion, a birthday party for Brazilian star footballer Ronaldo, one of the greatest players in the world, was indeed a surreal welcome. Beckham was not unfamiliar with glamour and excess (he was a star himself, as was his wife Victoria of the Spice Girls pop group) but this was something extraordinary.

Beckham had just begun his life as a Galactico, the name given to the superstar footballers of Réal Madrid, the Spanish team famous for signing the most well-known players on the planet. Tonight, was the beginning of Beckham's new life. Bernal, from Canberra in Australia, sucked in the night air and surveyed the scene unfurled in front of him: household names partying, kicking back in the privacy of Ronaldo's home. Here he was, a long way from his days as a part-time footballer in Australia where he worked as a park ranger to supplement his income. This night was the beginning of Bernal's new life, too.

As he watched international models dance with World Cup-winning stars, all friends of the Brazilian host, Bernal laughed at how quickly life can change. Two years before, he'd retired from football, calling quits on a playing career with English club Reading and little-known Spanish teams Jerez and Sporting Gijon. He'd taken up a job offer from SFX, a management company that included some of England's most well-known footballers on its books.

The job was straightforward. Use contacts he'd established from a decade in European football to drum up business for the management company. Bernal was also charged with finding young Australian kids to ship off to European clubs. He helped recruit Tim Cahill, the Socceroo who played for Everton in the English Premier League, to join SFX's stable of talent.

Bernal's fluent Spanish language skills would come in handy for SFX. David Beckham was the highest-profile client of the company's English office. When it was decided the star would move from Manchester United to Madrid, it was agreed Beckham – and SFX – would need a Spanish speaker to help find his way around the city. The London office scratched its collective head: Didn't that Bernal guy in Sydney speak Spanish?

On the morning of June 17, 2003, 36-year-old Bernal awoke in his Paddington apartment in Sydney's eastern suburbs and switched on his TV. A cable channel reported breaking news that David Beckham was on his way to Madrid. Bernal knew that, soon, he'd be too.

A day of email exchanges with SFX's London office saw Bernal kiss his young daughter goodbye and board a Cathay Pacific flight to London via Hong Kong. In London he was given his simple brief: cover Beckham's arse. Make sure Beckham gets whatever he wants. Make the star feel special. Look after him.

"The first few months will be trial and error," Bernal and his colleague Rebecca Loos were told. You've probably heard of Rebecca Loos. She's the woman who famously claimed to have had sex with Beckham in Madrid while his wife was out of town. But we're getting ahead of ourselves here...

Ronaldo's birthday party was strictly by invitation only. At the Brazilian's insistence, only Bernal and Loos were invited from Beckham's entourage (Bernal because he was a former professional footballer and Loos because, well, she was an attractive woman). Beckham and Bernal were at the Santo Mauro hotel at 9pm when team-mate Raul Bravo telephoned. Bravo, who had a brief spell playing in the English Premier League, could speak English.

"Boys, you really need to get yourself down here now," suggested the Réal Madrid defender.

Bravo was dead right.

"It was probably the greatest party I've ever been to," says Bernal. "And I was there babysitting Beckham."

But Beckham, as Bernal recalls, was undoubtedly one of the stars of the show. The party may have been for Ronaldo's birthday, but Beckham was the man of the moment, the newest Galactico, on show early in his Réal Madrid career.

"Even though there were a lot of well-known people there, every single person at that party turned around and looked at Beckham," says Bernal. "It was like he was glowing. As if a halo hung above his head."

If this story was a movie, it would not be Jerry Maguire, the Tom Cruise tale of a super-agent, with a big star client, who throws in his job for love. David Beckham may have had Rebecca Loos at hello but this is a story about a ruthless cyclone, a hurricane, a storm that blew across the centre of Spain, careering in and out, devouring whatever came into its path.

Beckham came to Madrid on July 1, 2003, to sign a $40 million contract. With paparazzi in pursuit, the traffic from Torrejon airport where private jets can take off and land, was chaos. Photographers and TV crews lined the streets. The welcome was presidential. The star's entourage, headed by a police motorbike escort, drove from Torrejon to the centre of town, where Bernal waited at a Madrid hospital while Beckham completed a medical before he could close the deal. Prodded and probed, Beckham was passed fit and signed on the dotted line.

Bernal then accompanied Beckham to the Fenix Melia Hotel, which straddles Madrid's Hard Rock Café (the Hard Rock would become a Beckham haunt). "We didn't tell anyone where we were going but half of Madrid seemed to be outside the hotel when we got there," Bernal recalls.

Beckham's wife, Victoria, was already at the Fenix Melia. A plate of sandwiches was brought to a room. Beckham decided he needed his ripped jeans sewn up. Housekeeping sent up a young worker who kneeled in front of Beckham and nervously stitched the rip as the most famous man in Madrid stood above her.

Then the group travelled to the famous Bernabeu stadium for photos and to finish formalities. Bernal kicked a ball with Beckham and son Brooklyn on the Bernabeu grass. Victoria, in a corridor overlooking the stadium, burst into tears. Beckham had arrived.

Rebecca Loos will forever be linked with Beckham's early days in Madrid. Not without reason. Beckham and Loos began to get friendly from day one out of necessity. There was no official office for Bernal and Loos to conduct Beckham's business so the task of managing the day to day affairs of the world's most well-known footballer was run from an internet café. Loos' father realised the ridiculousness of the situation and offered space at their family home outside Madrid.

The daily routine was soon set: Beckham would finish training late in the morning, Bernal and Loos would collect him, survive a car chase with paparazzi, collect a McDonalds lunch from a drive-through and head back to Loos' parent's house. Loos would swim in the pool, Beckham would lounge in the sun, and Bernal would try and work out how to connect his computer to the internet.

Idyllic days aside, with the attention Beckham received, it became clear extra security was needed. One of the first CVs Bernal saw was from Delfin Fernandez, a former Cuban government agent, recommended to Bernal by his friend, Spanish soap star Ana Obregon. Fernandez, explained Obregon, looked after actors Antonio Banderas and Penelope Cruz when they were in town. Forget the celebrity angle, Bernal thought. The Australian was impressed by one stand out client. Back in Cuba, Fernandez had spent years looking after Fidel Castro. Do the maths: 20 years, several assassination attempts, zero success. Castro was still alive, despite serious enemies. Fernandez was good. Very good. Beckham would get the best.

Bernal's daily life became more surreal. When not shuttling Beckham to training, he would sit with the star at long lunches alongside Réal Madrid's Brazilians Ronaldo and Roberto Carlos, fenced off from the public in the private rooms of Madrid's best restaurants. Bernal's social circle expanded to include Ana Obregon and legendary bull fighter Francisco Rivera, and Ana Cristina Fox, the daughter of the president of Mexico.

When Beckham wanted another Louis Vuitton bag to match the 20 he already had, Bernal would arrange for a store manager to visit Beckham at his hotel. As well as ensuring Beckham's 40 pairs of Adidas sneakers were treated with the respect they deserved, Bernal made sure Beckham's pet terrapins were well cared for.

There were car chases along mountain roads when a family drive became a cat and mouse game with the ever-present paparazzi and then there was Elton John. The singer would frequently call Beckham, sometimes for 10 minutes, sometimes for an hour.

"Yeah, yeah," Beckham would say to John.

"I know Elts…"

"It's hard Elts…"

"Love ya, Elts..."

Bernal and Loos would be with Beckham almost every minute of the day. When Victoria was out of town, they'd be the first people to see him in the morning and the last at night. And it was Bernal who unwittingly organised the dinner that led to Beckham and Loos making headlines.

Just days before Ronaldo's birthday party, after a photo shoot for one of Beckham's sponsors, Beckham, Bernal, Loos, SFX colleague, Andy Dart, a stylist called Maria Louise, and an English hairdresser called Ben, all went for dinner at a restaurant called Thai Gardens. The group eventually left the restaurant and moved on to the Ananda nightclub near Atocha railway station. Later, leaving the club, Beckham and Loos bundled into the lead vehicle, driven by Delfin Fernandez. Bernal later caught up with Fernandez at Beckham's hotel. After arriving, the Cuban went to the hotel security office and removed all video surveillance tapes. Fernandez was thorough. That was just how he did things.

Nothing was ever mentioned between anyone of what had happened that night. Not a word. Still, the apparent Beckham-Loos relationship exploded. British newspapers printed secretly-taken photos of Beckham and Loos together at the nightclub that night: Beckham had been spotted canoodling with a "mystery girl". Later, Loos would confess to an affair, denied by Beckham.

It was in the southern city of Valencia where Andy Bernal realised how badly organised his mission was. Réal Madrid had played a match against Valencia. Beckham had flown south with the team but Bernal made the four-hour journey in an Audi 8, one of Beckham's six cars. After the game, Beckham was to fly to London to link up with the England national team for a training camp. Bernal arranged to meet Beckham at Valencia's regular airport, where a Réal Madrid team bus would drop off their star. Bernal would then drive Beckham across town to catch a private jet to London.

Waiting at the airport, Bernal, received a text from Beckham: "We have to take one of the lads as well." No problem, thought Bernal.

The Madrid bus arrived. Beckham climbed into Bernal's passenger seat. The guy hitching a ride climbed in the back. Bernal turned and nodded hello. The lift was for Zinedine Zidane, the French World Cup star and another of the world's best players. Bernal shook with nerves as he pushed the car out into the traffic. He was carrying diamonds.

"What if I crash?" he thought. "What if someone hits me? What if these guys get hurt? There's about $250 million worth of talent in this car. I have the captain of England and the captain of France in my car and I don't even have a Spanish driver's licence." Bernal was driving Beckham around Spain on a New South Wales licence.

"Am I insured? I don't even have an employment contract."

Hands on the steering wheel at ten and two, Bernal looked straight ahead, and drove off slowly, with five words bouncing around his head: "What am I doing here?"

And then, almost as quickly as it began, it was over. On October 14, 2003, David Beckham released a statement that he'd ended his relationship with SFX but would continue to be represented by SFX agent Tony Stephens. If that appeared confusing, what was happening behind closed doors was total chaos.

The SFX machine was beginning to break down, not helped by the alleged relationship Loos - one of its employees - had with Beckham, now fully and controversially in the public spotlight, a situation SFX were certainly not keen to promote.

Bernal was called by SFX in London and told that things were "going to go down" the following day. Literally overnight, Madrid appeared to fill with people from 19 Management, the company that represented Victoria Beckham (and controls the Pop Idol, American Idol, and Australian Idol TV franchises).

Beckham's security team, hours earlier reliant on Bernal's inside knowledge of Madrid, attempted to ban the Australian from the Santa Mauro Hotel where Beckham was living. The irony: Bernal was trying to get into the hotel to attend a meeting, called by 19 Management, to discuss plans and whether Bernal would consider continuing to work for the England captain in Madrid. After that meeting, Bernal came face-to-face with Beckham and his wife at the hotel. Victoria was the ice queen. Beckham appeared embarrassed.

Bernal said to the star. "What's happening, David?"

Beckham was silent.

Victoria stepped in with words Bernal will never forget.

"Andy, we all have got mortgages to pay," she said, "We all got to do what we all got to do."

SFX were dumped. So, too, was Bernal.

The mission was over.

Well, perhaps it would be, if this was a movie. But this is real life. Beckham did call Bernal again before the Australian left Madrid. The Réal Madrid star explained he was at lunch, at a restaurant, with some of the girls from the new management team. Could Andy come out and join them? They needed some help translating the menu.

Bernal put down the phone and booked a flight back to Australia.

"It was madness," says Bernal.

IN JAPAN, NED ZELIC MISSES AUSTRALIA, BUT REGRETS NOTHING

Tokyo, November 2003

Regrets? Ned Zelic admits to a few but certainly not the decision to turn down a new contract with former club 1860 Munich and move to Japan. For many Australian fans, Zelic disappeared from the radar when he quit the Socceroos in 1999 after being dropped by Frank Farina for the then-rookie coach's second game in charge of the Socceroos. Zelic is enjoying a new lease of life in the J-League with Urawa Red Diamonds - one of the biggest clubs in Japan.

"I'd always been interested in playing in Japan ever since I came here with the national team in 1994," said Zelic. "I'd reached a stage where I'd played the Bundesliga for eight years. I was offered a new two-year deal at Munich but I never thought about signing it. I felt like I needed a total change."

Urawa Reds certainly offer that change for the much-travelled Zelic, whose former clubs include Borussia Dortmund and Eintracht Frankfurt in Germany, Queens Park Rangers in England, and Auxerre in France.

Urawa Red Diamonds, located in Saitama, north of Tokyo, are Japan's best supported-club with sell-out crowds of over 21,000 fans making the team the equal of many European sides. Owned by the Mitsubishi company, the team is coached by former Dutch national coach Hans Ooft and Wim Jansen, a member of Holland's 1974 World Cup side.

"So far, it's worked out well," said Zelic. "Of course, the big leagues of Europe are constantly in the spotlight, especially in Australia, but what many people don't understand is how much countries outside of Europe have improved. People could see that in the World Cup where there were a lot of surprises. The quality of football here in Japan has always been a good level. Not only with the Japanese players but good foreigners have come here to play and really boosted the standard."

"For Australia, it's always going to be difficult for soccer. In Japan, it was semi-professional and then all of a sudden, a lot of big companies came in and decided to pump huge amounts of money to get a league started and get good foreigners and good coaches. I can't see something like that happening in Australia, not in the short term, anyway."

Since his self-imposed Socceroo exile, it's often forgotten Zelic was considered one of Australia's greatest-ever players. His 1992 last-minute goal against Holland saw the Olyroos qualify for the Barcelona Olympics and formally reminded the world that soccer was played in Australia.

Zelic was snapped up by German giants Borussia Dortmund hours before Manchester United, on the verge of dominating the English Premier League, made an offer for his services. Zelic was also selected in a 1996 FIFA World XI.

"To help my country qualify for Olympics and secure a contract with a Bundesliga club on the same day was a fairytale," said Zelic. "I'm happy with the way my career progressed. I don't regret anything."

Not even quitting the Socceroos?

"I miss playing for the national team," Zelic said. "I miss it a lot but I don't regret the decision I made. I follow the team every time they play. There have been so many good times with them that it's disappointing the only thing people remember is me walking out."

"People criticised me for walking out on Australia but I wasn't doing that. I was walking out on a situation that I wasn't happy with. I've proven in the past that I'm a patriotic Australian who has put my spot at club level on the line to come back and play for my country. The reason I left was a misunderstanding, or whatever, with Frank. I don't want to say that I'll only come back if there's a coaching change. I can't ever see it happening. I still feel strongly about the decision."

TERRY ANTONIS IS 10 YEARS OLD BUT EVERYTHING WILL COME TRUE

Sydney, January 2004

Like most soccer crazy kids, Terry Antonis had a dream. The 10-year-old, from Georges Hall in Sydney's south-west, planned to line up for Australia alongside Socceroo Harry Kewell at the 2010 World Cup. He'd be 16 years old then. Don't laugh at his ambition. That's how you make it to the top.

First, though, there was the reality that Antonis faced the day I drove out to his home. The following week, the primary school kid was flying to Madrid for a training session with David Beckham.

In brief, Antonis was a freak. The kid's trip to train with Beckham was a prize won on a TV station competition, part of a global talent search for 20 young players to take part in a Beckham-backed coaching DVD. Remember DVDs? They used to find football talent.

Antonis, or rather his family, submitted an audition video that showed the young Sydneysider playing with a soccer ball as if he was a circus clown. It was no laughing matter, however, when Antonis casually added up his juggling record - the number of times he could kick a ball without it touching the ground. Over 5,800 times in a three-hour period. That was with a football. A tiny squash ball? Maybe 300 times before his mother called him in for dinner.

"I like soccer because it's fun," Antonis said. "I like training best because I get the ball more."

Antonis was introduced to football by his grandmother. His favourite position was centre midfield just like his hero, then Real Madrid's French wizard Zinedine Zidane.

"Réal Madrid are the best," Antonis said. "They have all the best players and they win the European Champions League."

They say that in show business you should never ever work with kids or animals. The same goes for journalism, but this kid clearly knew his stuff. He was unruffled by the prospect of meeting Beckham in Spain. After all, he did perform a juggling act in front of Harry Kewell and a massive crowd in Pitt Street Mall.

Antonis flew to Madrid with Angela Fimmano, another competition winner from Adelaide, for a whirlwind week. Although accompanied by family members, the official itinerary stated no parents or chaperones could attend the Beckham training session. Parents were told they wouldn't meet Beckham and no one could ask for autographs at the DVD shoot. Antonis was not worried by the strict rules.

"Maybe I can show David Beckham a few of my tricks," he said.

For Terry's father, Peter, the proudest moment would occur if his son one day pulls on a Socceroo shirt to represent his country. As well as his primary school team, Terry played with Sydney Olympic's Under-13 side, two years above his age group. Rather than flee Australia to sign with a European club, however, Peter Antonis hoped the new Australian Soccer Association would deliver his son a future at home.

"My dream would be for Terry to play for a team that represents all of Sydney in front of 30,000 crowds," he said. "I'd love my son to be able to entertain people and there would be nothing better than for him to do that at home."

There is, of course, a chasm between the dreams of a 10-year-old - even his father - and the reality of a professional football career. Branko Culina, Soccer NSW's Technical Director, hoped his plans to streamline and revolutionise youth coaching in NSW would help players like Terry Antonis realise their full potential.

"There's a big difference between a freak kid who has skills and what he does with those skills in years to come," Culina said. "It is phenomenal what Terry is able to do but the challenge is how to transform it to a game situation. I hope that along the way he comes across coaches that can harness his talent and assist it. It's important to encourage players like Terry Antonis and give them every opportunity to see how far he can go."

Postscript: Perhaps incredibly, everything Terry and his father Peter wished for came true.

WE HAVE ONE CAR BETWEEN US

Adelaide, May 2004

The cliché says that if it's 31-0 then this must be the Oceania Football Confederation World Cup qualifying competition but, thankfully, OFC took heed of record-breaking scores four years ago. A three-phase tournament saved teams such as American Samoa the embarrassment of massive drubbings against Australia. In 2001, the Samoans actually did watch 31 goals go past their goalkeeper.

This time around, Fiji, Vanuatu, Solomon Islands and Tahiti qualified from an earlier tournament to meet seeded Australia and New Zealand in a week-long competition in wintery Adelaide. In the South Pacific's version of Euro 2004, Tahiti took the drubbings (New Zealand beat them 10-0) but weren't necessarily the competition's fall guys. More on that later.

First, some perspective: the combined weekly income of Harry Kewell and Mark Viduka, Oceania's two biggest stars, far outstrips Vanuatu's entire annual football budget. In recent years, Vanuatu have come close to upsets against both Australia and New Zealand but run their national programme entirely on a US$250,000 grant from FIFA.

National team coach Carlos Buzzetti lived in Adelaide for 25 years before taking on the Vanuatu job and called in favours from old friends to ensure his team could compete against the regional giants. Adelaide faithfully adopted Buzzetti's squad - restaurants provided free meals and suburban soccer clubs hosted barbecues. The Australian team stayed in an award-winning city centre five-star hotel while Vanuatu's World Cup digs were a motel offering cut-price rates.

Another hurdle for the islanders was Adelaide's cold weather, not unusual for those Australians who play in Europe but a shock to Pacific residents. "My players wanted to stay in in bed all week because they didn't want to go outside in the cold," said Buzzetti.

OFC's decision to play a preliminary tournament to weed out weaker nations ironically proved a further financial burden on the region's poorer teams. "The qualifying tournament in Samoa in early May was a killer," Buzzetti explained. "Everything in Samoa was in US dollars and it cost us three times more than it usually does. We had to ask whether we could afford to compete in Adelaide."

Buzzetti's shoestring side are amateur but training schedules were helped by the poor local economy – no jobs meant most players could practice every day of the week. "I only have three players working and they maybe make $150 a month doing odd jobs," Buzzetti said. "We have one car between us and some of my players walk six kilometres to training. If I call for training twice a day then, well, you can imagine."

The ever-improving island nations made an otherwise tepid tournament interesting. Australia saw off New Zealand 1-0 in a turgid opener – played in front of just 11,000 spectators with no television coverage. Max Vieri, younger brother of Italy's Christian, made his debut for the Socceroos. Verdict: there are many reasons his brother has enjoyed more success.

Australia had relative pedigree (Tim Cahill and Mark Bresciano turned out for the Socceroos) but it was Buzzetti's boys who set the tournament alight with a convincing 4-2 win over New Zealand. The Kiwis, who were dire throughout, complained about a schedule that paired them with Australia first up. Yet the Aussies had come off tough warm-ups against Turkey while the All Whites had not played for six months.

Things got worse for New Zealand. The tournament's purpose was to find the top two sides, decided by a mini-league, to play off later in 2004 for a place at the 2005 Confederations Cup and then again in 2005 to find who will meet South America's fifth-placed side and qualify for Germany 2006.

Australia cruised into first place. The Solomons stole the second qualification spot with a 2-2 draw against the Australians. They will now play the Socceroos four times over the next 12 months. Kiwis could cry conspiracy but the reality was that Australia's defence, shorn of Rangers captain Craig Moore and Crystal Palace's Tony Popovic, was appalling against the Solomons.

The streets of Honiara, the Solomons capital on the island of Guadalcanal, were packed with celebrating fans. Soccer is the number one sport in the country, something only Tahiti can also claim in Oceania.

SHINY AND NEW: FRANK LOWY DREAMS OF SYDNEY, NEW ZEALAND, AND ASIA

Sydney, March 2004

You can't blame him for being optimistic. On Frank Lowy's to-do list when he was parachuted into Australian soccer's top job - as chairman of the Australian Soccer Association (my emphasis) - was for the proposed new "Australian Premier League" to expand into an Asian-Pacific club championship and include teams from Australia, New Zealand, and Asia. Well, he got the team from New Zealand.

In his first one-on-one interview after deciding to take on the job of fixing football in Australia, Frank Lowy sat in his East Sydney office and laid out his blueprint for the new league. He called on Australian players in Europe to return home to play in the new league. He also sent a blunt public message to his new CEO John O'Neill - deliver the goods. At the time, it seemed starry eyed. In retrospect, context is everything. It seemed like a good idea at the time.

"We have a plan to play in Asia," Lowy said. "It would be something like the Asian Champions League. Soccer is thriving in most parts of Asia and we ought to plug into that and New Zealand."

Lowy said the first step in establishing an Asian competition would be to grant a New Zealand team entry into the proposed Australian Premier League. Under the plan, the Australian competition would then bloom into an Asian-Pacific super league or run parallel with a future inter-continental competition. The Asian Football Confederation has run its own Asian Club championship since 1967 with teams included from Japan, South Korea, China, and Saudi Arabia.

Lowy said the key to an Asian-Pacific tournament would be television backing. To help with that, Lowy appointed Ian Frykberg, a former rugby league Super League boss and ex-News Limited

Director of Sport, as his television consultant.

"We need to establish the league here with one team from New Zealand so that we have a trans-Tasman leg," Lowy said. "Once we have established that, and it's working, we will look to have a league or a competition which will embrace international teams from our region. It is one of our objectives. This will be driven by television. We can create a competition that is meaningful in Asia."

Lowy conceded the new league will initially struggle to match player salaries on offer, even in Europe's low-profile competitions, but called on Australians playing in smaller European leagues to return home. Lowy made a personal plea to Paul Okon - currently playing in Belgium's second division - as well as out-of-contract Ned Zelic to return to play in the new Australian competition.

"I have a message to those players," Lowy said. "They should come home. We need to pay them accordingly but it's also in their interest. If those players succeed in getting us to the World Cup then the game will be bigger here. I would like them to earn a lot more but that will depend on how good the game is and how many spectators we get."

The Westfield boss said he was unable to commit to a start date for the new league but indicated the most feasible kick-off would be early next year. He acknowledged some players would face career limbo over the next nine months. Contracts for current National Soccer League players become void on June 30 with the NSL's top players likely to sign contracts in Europe or Asia that will rule them out of the new league's debut season.

"There is a problem but I understand," Lowy said. "I don't have a magic wand but people need to be a little bit understanding. The issues are complex. There is 20 or 30 years of mismanagement of the game. Establishing the new league will be the toughest job."

While Perth, Adelaide, and Melbourne had strong consortiums bidding for places in the new league, there was been little noise from prospective Sydney teams. Lowy, however, was confident Sydney will be a force in the competition.

"Sydney is a very important and there is no doubt we will get the team we want in Sydney," he said. "We can't rest easy but we will have proper representation for Sydney."

Lowy would surrender his role as executive chairman when John O'Neill began work at ASA's Homebush headquarters and said he expected the former Australian Rugby Union boss to transform Australian soccer into a local sporting powerhouse.

"We have expectations on him to deliver," Lowy said. "The board and chairman can't run the ASA. It needs a full-time person, full commitment, with a knowledge of sport and the commercial world. The hard work starts now."

"O'Neill does not have to be a soccer expert. It might be an advantage not to have prejudgment about things. It is not enough to be an enthusiast, a sports supporter, to be a good administrator."

THAT TIME AUSTRALIAN FOOTBALL WAS GOING TO BUY A PREMIER LEAGUE CLUB

Sydney, May 2004

Australian Soccer Association CEO John O'Neill had a bold plan. The Australian federation would invest in a British football club. Full points for big ideas. The problem was the idea was received by local insiders with a mixture of confusion and amusement.

Two months into his tenure as the local game's boss the O'Neill scheme was a vision of Harry Kewell, Mark Viduka, Stan Lazaridis, and Mark Schwarzer all playing for an ASA-owned English Premier League club. A former boss of the Australian Rugby Union, O'Neill explained the plan as a way of avoiding club versus country conflict and "opening up a new world for Australian soccer as far as media and media exposure through TV rights is concerned."

But the left-field idea only made Australia's soccer cognoscenti, who welcome a radical revamp of the local league, scratch its head at O'Neill's version of a global vision.

"The reason the United States and Japanese national teams are successful are because they have got their local leagues in order," said Steve Horvat, a former Socceroo who is behind a Melbourne bid for Australia's new domestic competition. "It is paramount that we get our own backyard in order before considering overseas ventures.

One national team player said: "It's not even worthy of a comment."

O'Neill's plan was seen as a slap in the face for the mooted new domestic league, with claims any money the ASA may have at its disposal should be invested locally.

"Some careful and efficient planning will avoid club versus country dilemmas at zero cost," said Leo Karis, a FIFA player agent and soccer marketing expert.

"Plan Socceroo games on FIFA designated weeks in Europe and there will be no clash with clubs. If we're considering investing $1 million in a British club then let's instead invest $10 million in the local league. We can attract very good players to Australia if the ASA invests properly in a local league. A $10 million investment by the Australian Soccer Association will get 80 players back to Australia and that will significantly change the standard and, possibly, attract commercial TV interest. If the culture is to keep players in Australia then the investment in a foreign club promotes the export of local talent, the very opposite of what we should be encouraging."

Even in 2004, foreign investment was not unusual in European soccer. Chelsea is owned by Roman Abramovich, the billionaire Russian oil tycoon, while Thailand's government is attempting to buy a 30 per cent stake in Liverpool valued at US$113 million. O'Neill is also understood to have discussed with ASA chairman Frank Lowy the difficulty of launching of a viable domestic league.

O'Neill's announcement came after abandoning the Professional Footballer's Association plan for an Australian Premier League - the PFA holds the rights to the APL name - in favour of his own vision for a domestic competition.

If the ASA does raise a white flag on the new league and instead focus on overseas investment, one mooted plan would be to set up a club as an academy for Australian youth development. The ASA would buy a lower league European club and flood its playing roster with the best young Australian talent, later on-selling successful players to bigger clubs at profit.

"It's not a very original idea," said Bernie Mandic, manager of Socceroo star Harry Kewell. "The key to success is not how grand the vision is but how small and precise it is. If the ASA is serious about this plan, then it must only get involved in a small club."

Postscript: As history shows, this big idea died the day after the story appeared in the newspaper .

TIM CAHILL, "THE SITUATION", AND HIS ARRIVAL IN THE PREMIER LEAGUE

Liverpool, September 2004

There was an air of, if not disbelief, then at least quiet surprise around Goodison Park after Sunday's win over Middlesbrough lifted Everton into the Premiership's top three. Speaking to the media after the match, David Moyes gave a fair impression of a rabbit caught in headlights. The questions about what happens to an Everton shorn of Wayne Rooney have now stopped. Instead, the grilling is all about what Everton are doing at the right end of the table - in third place.

Relegation battle? No. A challenge for European places? Come back in May, but for now this Everton side are a sweet example of application and teamwork outweighing the influence of individuals.

This has been apparent to Tim Cahill, who arrived at Goodison Park from Millwall in August just as Rooney was looking for the exit. Rather than operate as a home to the stars, Everton, Cahill suggests, now wield an us-against-them spirit similar to that which flowed through Millwall.

"Last week's win against Middlesbrough was a great result and I'm just really, really happy for the lads and for the club," he said. "I wouldn't have signed here if I didn't think this was a massive club capable of going places, but we must keep improving. All the ingredients are there. All the lads here are down to earth, and they made it easy for me to settle in, but the difference in standard between here and Millwall is massive. Here the players are strong, physically and mentally. They're great footballers with that extra edge. Everything you do in the Premiership is under a microscope. You need to do well all the time. There's a lot of pressure on players coming into a league like this."

For Cahill, pressure is a good thing. Not that motivation is missing for the 24-year-old. He has played only two Premiership matches for Everton, first because of his commitments at the Olympic

Games with Australia and second because he was suspended for the Middlesbrough match for what is now known at Goodison Park as "the situation" - he was sent off for pulling up his shirt, celebrating a match-winning first goal for his new club against Manchester City a fortnight ago.

Cahill has a track record with exuberance. After scoring Millwall's opener against Sunderland in last season's FA Cup semi-final the midfielder ran the length of Old Trafford waving his shirt above his head to seek out family and friends who had travelled from Australia for the game.

"I might get into controversy, but it can't be helped," said Cahill. "I just show my emotions as a footballer. Especially scoring goals. The first one for Everton meant a lot to me. I don't regret it. It's just something that I've always done when I've celebrated. Everyone was bemused by it and it was nice of Sepp Blatter to come out and back me as well. That meant a lot."

"Everyone said that I was Forrest Gump with my shirt off. My emotions were running crazy and I was looking for my family in the crowd. The fact that it was my goal that got us to the final made it even more unbelievable."

Cahill literally burst into wider football consciousness with Millwall's run to the 2004 FA Cup Final. In what would become a career of big games, he told me the week prior to the final against Manchester United that the game would be his "biggest game ever".

"This is the biggest moment and the biggest stage of my career and my biggest game ever," he said. "This is the biggest competition in the world, watched on TV by 500 million people. This is definitely what it's all about."

At 24 years old, he'd certainly mastered the fine art of hyperbole.

The London side were underdogs but Cahill said Millwall were confident of pulling off an upset against a United team that was searching for its sole trophy that season. Cahill faced a duel with Roy Keane in midfield.

"I can't wait to meet Roy Keane but I don't think my introduction will be a handshake," Cahill said. "We fancy our chances. This is the worst form Man United have ever been in for a while. Still, even on their worst days they're still one of the best teams in the world so it won't be easy. They haven't won anything this season and they need to win this cup."

Millwall's other Socceroo, defender Kevin Muscat, would miss the final after badly injuring his knee in a tackle against Sunderland. Cahill said Millwall, known as the Lions, were using the absence of Muscat, and suspended striker Danny Dichio, as inspiration.

"We'll go up a gear for them," Cahill said. "They played a big part all year, Danny with his goals and Muskie as a leader. Kevin has been such an influence and has had a massive part to play in this."

United's cup final line-up included Gary Neville, Ryan Giggs, Paul Scholes, Ruud Van Nistelrooy, the American goalkeeper Tim Howard, Cristiano Ronaldo, and Ole Gunnar Solskjaer. The match was Cahill's last game for Millwall. United won 3-0. From kick-off, Millwall were never in it.

Still, although the celebrations belonged to a shirtless Cristiano Ronaldo for that game, Cahill's explosive highs elsewhere perhaps had roots in the long path he took to the Premiership. Like several Australians before him, he left Sydney as a teenager and arrived raw at Millwall to develop into a midfield centrepiece for last season's overachievers.

He made his debut for Australia in March 2004, as a substitute against South Africa in a London friendly, after a 10-year exile from international football. A substitute appearance for Western Samoa, his mother's birthplace, as a 14-year-old visiting his grandmother had seemingly ended his Socceroos career before it began.

The Samoans were prepared to surrender Cahill to Australia but FIFA was immovable until new regulations were introduced at the beginning of 2004, inspired by Cahill's campaign. He seemed likely to become a crucial cog in Frank Farina's midfield.

"I'm definitely an emotional player," he said. "Not just if I score a goal. I'm just really passionate and just want to do really well and work as hard as I can. Being in the Premiership I now have to take every opportunity and be thankful for the position I'm in. I do believe in giving 100 percent every time. I don't see the point in going out there and being half-hearted. You'd never forgive yourself."

And what of Merseyside's other Australian, Liverpool's hot-and-cold Harry Kewell? Cahill sees no competition with his international team-mate nor a need to eclipse Kewell.

"I don't want to do that and I don't want to bring all the attention to myself," he said. "Harry is obviously a massive icon here and in Australia but that's because he's a good footballer. I want to just be happy playing."

Cahill believes that success is about graft not glamour: "You just have to put in a good shift. I like to think that I'm very disciplined and can work hard. If good things happen then fair enough. If it doesn't then you have to go back to the drawing board and start again."

JOHNNY WARREN, THE BEAT OF BOSSA NOVA, AND SAUDADE

Sydney, November 2004

There is one enduring image of Johnny Warren. On November 29, 1997, his beloved Socceroos had just lost the two-match qualifying play-off for a place at the 1998 World Cup finals. Opponents Iran had snatched a desperate and dramatic 2-2 draw with Australia to qualify by the away-goal rule.

Warren, at that time part of the only Australian team to play at a World Cup in 1974, faced the country's television viewers in his role as a match analyst. Anchor Les Murray asked his close friend and colleague how he viewed the result.

Warren tried to speak to the millions watching. Instead, he spoke for them. Rather than give a blow-by-blow dissection of Iran's heart-breaking goals he simply mumbled words of despair and broke down in tears. Johnny Warren was a World Cup player, coach, administrator, agitator, media commentator and Australian icon. More significantly, he was one of us.

Warren was born in Sydney and grew up in the suburb of Botany. Also a talented young cricketer, he was rejected for his local under-12 soccer team at *the age* of nine, legend now suggesting that he was too small and needed to go home and eat more porridge.

He must have digested a lot of oats. A year later he made his first appearance for a representative soccer team when he played for the New South Wales Protestant Churches side at *the age* of 10. At 16, he was playing against adults for Canterbury's senior first team and one year later established himself as a genuine star in the NSW state competition, the highest domestic level for the sport at the time. In 1963 he joined St George-Budapest, a team formed by Hungarian immigrants that became one of the country's biggest soccer clubs, to begin what would be a history-making 12-year stint with the club.

Warren's playing career ended before the National Soccer League was established in 1977 and it was with the national team that he took the first steps in becoming a household name. In the 1960s, Australia's soccer pulse was beating with the blood of newly arrived immigrants from Britain and the rest of Europe. In his sporting community, Skippy Warren was almost an alien in his own country. But just as the Aboriginal activist Charlie Perkins had been warmly embraced by Sydney's Greek community during his own playing career with the Pan-Hellenic club in the 1960s, so was the Aussie Warren championed by the so-called new Australians.

Warren made his debut for Australia in 1965 in an era when dreams of a lucrative contract in Europe's glamour leagues just didn't occur. The playing fields were Cambodia, Hong Kong, Rhodesia and Israel. During his time as a Socceroo, the pioneering national team was a mélange of immigrants, a mixture of languages and accents, sprinkled with a few Australian-born players. This team was before its time, representative of a future Australia. With the Aboriginal Harry Williams in the side, it was the only sporting team to truly reflect the country's diverse social make-up.

Warren was appointed captain of the national team in 1967, the same year that the Australian government sent the team to play in Vietnam as part of a wartime international public relations exercise. It couldn't do that with rugby league, cricket or Australian rules, Warren would later recall. The seed of Warren's soccer internationalism was sown.

It's often thought that the crowning moment of Warren's playing career was Australia's appearance at the 1974 World Cup but his role in that team was limited by injury. Australia's qualification was remarkable given the team was made up of part-timers - some delivery drivers and painters even had to ask for time off to play in the finals in Germany. Qualification was even more remarkable given that just 16 teams took part in a competition that has doubled in the number of participating teams in recent years.

Warren played just one match of Australia's three games - against East Germany - a foot injury ruling him out of most of the tournament. That he made the team at all was a sign of his later resilience. A knee injury in 1970 had put him out of the sport for 15 months during which time he lost the Socceroo captaincy to Peter Wilson. But Warren made a comeback and coach Rale Rasic realised he could not leave the attacking midfielder out of his squad. He retired after the World Cup, having made 62 appearances for Australia, and filling his passport with stamps from all corners of the world.

Brazil became Warren's spiritual home. He fell in love, not just with the South American attitude to football, but with the entire spirit of the continent. He was consumed by that spirit. Brazilians call it saudade. Almost untranslatable, the closest meaning suggests perhaps a nostalgia, a longing, for somewhere else, a place far away. Its themes run through bossa nova, Brazil's homegrown take on jazz popularised by Joao Gilberto and Tom Jobim. It was bossa nova, with saudade, rather than the clichés of samba that would provide a soundtrack for Warren's life. He was in love with football but was shrouded in melancholy.

The heartbreak was this: the boy from Botany wished he could have been born deep in the favelas of Rio de Janeiro, São Paulo, or by the beaches of Porto Alegre, rather than Bondi. Warren's deep longing was that football - we won't dare call it soccer - the world game, would be embraced by fellow Australians. After his playing career ended, he made it his zealous mission to convert the unwashed. Warren saw himself dancing at a metaphorical Rio carnevale. He wanted us all at the party.

If grassroots participation numbers, the enthusiasm generated by television coverage of the 2002 World Cup and nervous administrators of the other football codes are anything to go by, Warren almost succeeded. Soccer may not have been the dominant sport in Australia during his lifetime but its momentum, much generated by his evangelism, was now unstoppable.

Warren would sometimes joke he'd be able to walk into the offices of Afghanistan's football authorities during the height of the Taliban regime and be greeted with open arms. The thing was he wasn't really joking. The myth of Johnny Warren's international legend loomed large but it was seen first-hand in the corridors of the massive Stade de France before the 1998 World Cup Final between France and Brazil. Warren was in the company of the powerful and great of world football but there were no diplomatic, polite handshakes, rather the hugs of brotherhood. Australia may be an insignificant minnow within the world's most popular sport but Captain Socceroo was welcomed as one of the family.

For the statisticians: in 1974, Warren was made a Member of the Order of the British Empire (MBE) for services to soccer; he coached Canberra City in the National Soccer League; he was inducted in the Australian Sports Hall of Fame in 1986 and the Australian Soccer Hall of Fame in 1999; he had the medal for the National Soccer League's player of the year named after him; this year he was awarded the very select FIFA Centenary Order of Merit by the world governing body's president, Sepp Blatter, in a ceremony in Sydney.

Les Murray has described Warren as a Nelson Mandela for Australian soccer fans but the statue of Christ The Redeemer that towers over Rio de Janeiro is a more appropriate comparison. Warren transcended his sport.

An afterlife can be a matter for conjecture but one thing is certain: if rugby likes to consider itself the game played in heaven, with Warren newly arrived that's no longer likely to be the case.

FRANK FARINA FIGHTS FIRES (AND OTHER PART TIME JOBS FOR A NATIONAL TEAM COACH)

Sydney, August 1999

As a professional footballer, Frank Farina knew it didn't matter how you won. It just mattered that you won. And so it was in 1999 that Farina was appointed national coach after two preferred candidates were ruled out in deals aimed at placating opposing camps on Soccer Australia's dysfunctional board.

There were four contenders to take over from Terry Venables after the failed 1998 World Cup campaign. Eddie Krncevic and David Mitchell were former Socceroos who, like Farina, had recently returned from pioneering playing careers in Europe. And like Farina, they had impressive starts to their coaching career with National Soccer League clubs in Australia.

Also in the mix was Ange Postecoglou, another young NSL coach without the extensive European playing career of the other three. The Soccer Australia board would decide who was the best coach to take the reins of the national team. Whether they were experts in finding an elite coach is not known but they were very good at deciding on the future of the sport by making deals with each other.

The candidates made presentations to the board. Some did their own work, others had help from trusted confidantes in navigating PowerPoint and filling binders with football philosophy and tactical analysis. In the first round of voting, Krncevic and Mitchell scored two votes each from Soccer Australia's five-man board. Farina just one, while Postecoglou failed to rate.

The candidates' phones ran hot. Both Mitchell and Krncevic were told they'd won the top job. In truth, the battle had not yet begun. Not for the first time, nor for the last, fast deals were done. Soccer Australia allegiances shifted. Compromise was reached. Farina now found himself with three votes and the winning candidate. Krncevic was promised a coaching job at NSL club Marconi - Farina's current job. Postecoglou was named coach of national youth teams. Mitchell was cast aside. All of that happened behind closed doors. Unlike Farina's fall – which happened very much in public.

Crete, August 2004

The campaign to topple Frank Farina as Socceroo coach went up a gear yesterday with French legend Manuel Amoros formally informing the Australian Soccer Association of his availability and Bruno Metsu, Senegal's upstart coach at the 2002 World Cup, flagging interest in the Australia job.

As Farina made a heartfelt case for his defence prior to his Olympic team's crunch group game against Serbia and Montenegro in Crete overnight, ASA boss John O'Neill received a letter from Amoros where the former French captain expressed interest in any position with the ASA, including the top job leading the Socceroos.

O'Neill has left Sydney for Athens to rendezvous with ASA chairman Frank Lowy before a scheduled meeting with the England Football Association in London. The ASA boss denied a widely mooted meeting with former Liverpool boss Gerard Houllier was scheduled on his European trip.

Since ASA's flirtation with Houllier became public, other international coaches have flagged interest in the Australia job. Widely-respected Metsu has told agents that if Houllier is being considered for any role with Australia then he too must be a consideration.

Farina, in the middle of the Olympic football tournament, said he was disappointed by developments and suggested there was a cloak and dagger campaign to unseat him.

"It's poor timing and maybe people are playing funny buggers," Farina said. "It's poor form to do this for the pressure it puts on the team. It's a little bit unfair. Every tournament for the last three years, every time we've played a game, it's been the same old, same old

There are other things behind it. The politics continue."

Farina said he had copped unfair criticism over Australia's 2-2 Oceania Nations Cup draw with the Solomon Islands earlier in the year, a result that will see the Socceroos play the island nation four times over the next 12 months rather than money-maker New Zealand.

Farina had also been told expectations for the Olympic team had recently risen when, he recalled, earlier this year the no-frills squad was rated the worst ever Australian Olympic team.

"Six months ago this was the worst Olympic team ever, they've played four international games since, and now they have to win a medal," Farina said. "On what grounds are those expectations based? Someone must explain how you go from being the worst team to having to win a medal or you're a failure. It is totally unfair on the players."

"The Solomon Islands game is being thrown around all the time," said Farina. "When we beat Vanuatu, we knew we'd won the tournament, we had no chance of losing and, as any international coach would do, once it was wrapped up, I gave a run to the Olympic team players we had in the squad."

"We got a 2-2 draw which no one was happy about but if anyone from ASA had said we had to win this game and it was vitally important that we play New Zealand in World Cup and Confederation Cup qualifiers, then it would have been different. I would have said to Tony Vidmar that he couldn't go back to Britain and see his newborn kid. I would have pushed Lazaridis, Grella, and Bresciano to play and I wouldn't have gone with my Olympic back line. The criticism is part of my job. It's the same old faces bringing it up. They will continue to do it and there's nothing I can do about it."

Innsbruck, January 2005

Exiled Socceroo Ned Zelic has sent a public call to Frank Farina for a sit-down meeting to discuss a national team comeback. Zelic said he'd welcome clear-the-air talks with Farina after the national coach expressed fears of striking out for a third time attempting to lure the talented defender back to the Socceroos.

"Let's talk," Zelic said. "I don't care if it's on the phone or face to face. I want to play for my country. That is the truth. But before that happens Frank and I obviously have to discuss a few things."

Zelic controversially quit the Socceroos in 1999 after being dropped for Farina's second game in charge of Australia against Brazil's under-23 side in Melbourne. Farina made two unsuccessful attempts to lure Zelic back to the fold in 2001 and does not want a third rejection if the Australian legend is not serious about a comeback. Zelic hosed down suggestions his exile had been because of a feud with Farina and said it was time to put history behind them.

"I love playing for Australia," Zelic said. "I always did. For me to walk away was not an easy decision. Five years down the track I now feel that I can help my country. I don't have a problem with Frank as a person. We got on well when we both played with the national team. Frank was someone who I always felt comfortable with. I had a problem with what happened in 1999. I reacted when he told me I would not be playing. It infuriated me and I exploded and blew up. I just expected a bit more from him."

Zelic said a supposed rivalry with Paul Okon, recently dumped as Socceroo captain, played no part in his decision to quit the team nor now consider a comeback.

"Would I walk away if Paul Okon was recalled to the team again?" he said. "No. We played together when Australia qualified against Holland for the Barcelona Olympics. We never met up at the hotel bar to have a beer but neither were we ready to put the gloves on."

Zelic, now 33, said the opportunity to talk with Farina would allow both parties to judge if a comeback would suit both player and coach.

"Walking out was a one-off situation," Zelic said. "Time heals wounds. Both parties have to be committed to the cause. I have to know that Frank wants me and needs me. If he has other things in mind, then I respect that. I'm not saying I'm only coming back if Frank picks me for every game and I play 90 minutes but we have to sort some things out. I have shown in the past, with the sacrifices I've made, that I've been committed to the cause. I've always been committed when it has come to playing for my country."

Farina leaves for an extended stint in Europe later this month which will allow the opportunity for a face-to-face meeting with Zelic - now playing for Austrian first division team Wacker Tirol - before Australia play South Africa on February 9.

"You should not have to twist a player's arm to play for Australia," Farina said. "I want players who are determined to play. Tim Cahill told me he didn't care if he was in the team, in the squad, he just wanted to be there."

Postscript: Farina did not recall Zelic.

Sydney, February 2005

Football Federation Australia boss John O'Neill has sounded a ringing endorsement of coach Frank Farina ahead of the Socceroos match with South Africa this week. O'Neill, FFA chief executive officer, was speaking to end speculation about Farina's position following several high-profile coaching candidates expressing interest in the Australia job.

"Frank Farina's job is assured," O'Neill said.

"He has a contract that's been in place since the end of the last World Cup campaign that goes through to the end of the current campaign."

O'Neill said Farina is safe in his position until Australia bows out of the World Cup, either in November after the qualifier play-offs or next year in Germany.

"The contract is specific," O'Neill said. "It expires at the end of our World Cup campaign. If we don't qualify in November that's the end of our campaign. We don't want to distract the coach. We want a coach who has job security and can get on with it. We must all be singing from the same hymn sheet."

FFA has received recent interest in Farina's position from former Fulham and Monaco coach Jean Tigana. Last year, former French World Cup captain Manuel Amoros expressed a desire for the job after flying from France to watch Australia play Turkey. Amoros has now moved into the box seat as possible coach of A-League club Sydney FC. Up to four CVs a week arrive in the FFA mailbox from coaches interested in the head coaching position.

"We have certainly had a mixed bag of applications," O'Neill said.

O'Neill said significant speculation about Farina's position had also come from FFA's search for a potential Technical Director. Former Blackburn Rovers and Inter Milan coach Roy Hodgson, current Scotland boss Walter Smith, and former Southampton manager Gordon Strachan were all considered candidates.

"We were talking to those people about the Technical Directors' job and that became a presumption we were about to replace the coach," O'Neill said. "That was not the case."

O'Neill said Farina and the Socceroos faced unique hurdles in qualifying for the World Cup. Those current circumstances were previously accompanied by poor organisation and preparation that hindered past World Cup campaigns. He added that Australia benefited from Farina's experience in South America in 2001.

"Farina is a much better coach and a better person from his experiences over the past four years," O'Neill said. "If you're half-smart you go into the next occasion a lot better off. Frank has a very difficult road to hoe. His match schedule has previously been a dog's breakfast. He had absent players. The infrastructure has been zero. We have fixed the infrastructure and we have a match schedule that's worthwhile. The stars are aligned better for Frank than they have been in the past."

Farina now faces the unusual situation of preparing for the match against South Africa without speculation over his position. He claimed the 2004 Athens Olympic campaign had been marred by rumours over his position that disrupted the team.

Sydney, March 2005

Football Federation Australia boss John O'Neill has denied the governing body has plans to sack Frank Farina if the Socceroo coach is charged with assault. O'Neill said FFA was awaiting the result of a police investigation into the now-infamous encounter between Farina and an SBS-TV reporter before making its next move on the issue.

"I can categorically deny we have a contingency plan should Frank be charged with assault," O'Neill said. "We do not want to go down the path of future implications at this stage."

New South Wales police are understood to have enough evidence to lay charges against Farina, having received statements from witnesses to the incident between Farina and reporter Andrew Orsatti in the tunnel after Australia's recent friendly with Iraq. Witnesses include employees from SBS, production crew from outside broadcast company Zero1Zero, stadium staff, and Football Federation Australia officials.

O'Neill said no FFA employees had yet been interviewed by police although media manager Stuart Hodge, a key witness to events, has sent a statement to investigating detectives.

"I'd be surprised if [police do have enough evidence] as they haven't interviewed any FFA people yet," O'Neill said. "A significant number of FFA people were witnesses. I would expect them to be interviewed by police. Of course, we are cooperating. It is a serious matter and it is not being taken lightly."

The police investigation will not be concluded until at least April 18 when the detective leading the case returns from leave. Both FFA and SBS have opened separate investigations into the tunnel incident. The Media Arts Entertainment Alliance, the journalists union, is also looking at the post-match events.

"As a general principle, we are very concerned by any assault on journalists," said MEAA Federal Secretary Christopher Warren. "People think it can be trivial but it is a serious matter."

"There were 129 journalists killed last year. The climate of violence against journalists is one of the great dangers of press freedom whether it's by a footballer, a rock star, or a dictator."

Witness statements include descriptions of the altercation as the Socceroo coach was on his way to a post-match press conference. What is not in dispute is that Orsatti challenged Farina about short answers during an earlier post-match TV interview, part of an SBS broadcast agreement with FFA. Orsatti is alleged to have said: "What the fuck was all that about?"

An altercation followed, after which Orsatti told Farina: "You're unbelievable - we're in this together."

Farina is alleged to have responded: "We're not in this together. You're against me."

Witnesses also claim two further incidents occurred after FFA media manager Stuart Hodge intervened in the alleged initial clash.

The incident occurred just minutes before visiting dignitaries, including Prime Minister John Howard, Asian Football Confederation President Mohamed bin Hammam, and FFA Chairman Frank Lowy made a visit to Australia and Iraq's dressing rooms. The incident has complicated relations between FFA and SBS. The television network is the rights holder to national team matches but has fallen from Farina's favour for critical analysis of the national team's performances.

John O'Neill said Farina had been spoken to about his attitude in recent post-match interviews with SBS. "I have counselled him about the interviews he did with SBS after the game in South Africa and Iraq," O'Neill said. "We have obligations to SBS."

Farina and SBS had a long history. A few years earlier Farina was about to be interviewed by Les Murray and Johnny Warren, when seconds before going live Farina said the TV duo reminded him of Waldorf and Statler, characters from The Muppets.

Frankfurt, July 2005

Turmoil. Disarray. Chaos. Words once easily associated with soccer in Australia. The sacking of national team coach Frank Farina inspired many to wrap the sport in those terms once more. They needn't have. Instead, Football Federation Australia chairman Frank Lowy and CEO John O'Neill ignored the Aussie maxim that "she'll be right". As the Confederations Cup in Germany last month revealed - when Australia lost all three of its games - things were clearly wrong.

"We're only playing for ourselves," whispered a Socceroo before the Confederations Cup, a dress rehearsal for next year's FIFA World Cup, had even kicked off. The hint was that some star players no longer had faith in the ability of Farina to ensure the team returned to Germany next year for the World Cup.

Watching the Socceroos in action in Germany at the Confederations Cup, Frank Lowy agreed with that player's assessment and used his time well. The Westfield boss moves in such influential circles within world football that even John O'Neill was not affronted when he initially couldn't get past security to join his boss at a VVIP function in Frankfurt.

The plan of succession was so well executed that this week FFA officials returned to Europe to finalise the new coach's contract. With no Australian considered talented enough the only real question is whether to seek a long-term solution or hire someone just to beat the as yet unknown fifth-placed South American team in its World Cup qualifying play-off this November.

Former England coaches Glenn Hoddle and Kevin Keegan have been suggested but those once great players struggle to get jobs in their own country (England's national team coach is Swedish, the top Premier League coaches are Scottish or European). Former two-time Holland coach Dick Advocaat is a front runner but there's also the "Johnny Warren Solution": an argument Australia should finally appoint a South American coach, especially considering our 2006 World Cup path.

"Australia needs a big fish that has experience at the top level in South America," says Andrew Bernal, a former Socceroo who has also worked for international sports management giant SFX and was David Beckham's personal minder when the superstar signed for Real Madrid. Bernal also recently worked as a scout for the FFA in South America, gathering intelligence on potential World Cup play-off opponents.

"The new coach must fully comprehend the beast we're up against," Bernal says. "We need a leader of men and a motivator. A coach who our star players can look up to, respect, and most importantly, want to play for."

More motivation for Lowy to think big is that Australia's football future no longer hinges on four-yearly World Cup qualification (or failure). Amid the Farina fracas, a far more monumental event occurred last week in Frankfurt when Australia's move to the Asia Football Confederation was rubber stamped by FIFA.

As of January 1, 2006, the Socceroos no longer face oblivion if things go loco in November. Instead, Australia, led by a high-profile international coach, will play regular and lucrative tournaments with teams that include Japan, South Korea, China, and Arab nations. Very soon, Frank Farina will be little more than an encyclopedia entry while turmoil, disarray, and chaos will be lost in translation.

Amsterdam, July 2005

Football Federation Australia officials head to Europe this week with the knowledge the vacant Socceroo coaching position is currently world football's most-wanted job. FFA Head of High Performance John Boultbee leads the headhunting mission with a bulging bag of job applications. However, it is known a shortlist of new coaches was drawn up before Frank Farina received the axe and the trip is to seal a deal with one of a select group of candidates. Boultbee said that FFA's fax machine began humming with hopeful CVs just 30 minutes after Farina's sacking was made public.

"The first application came in from England within half an hour of the announcement on Wednesday," Boultbee said. "We have received a long list people who have sent in applications as well as a list of suggestions from people and had a number of agents who have called claiming to represent the most fantastic coaches in the world. It is amazing. There are some are significant names among them and some less significant. There are a lot of football coaches around, that's for sure."

FFA bosses remain tight-lipped about Farina's successor but the pack is led by heavyweight Dutchman Dick Advocaat, a former coach of Holland and Scottish club Rangers, and a relative unknown in Frenchman Christian Damiano. Damiano was recommended for a role with the FFA three months ago by ex-Liverpool boss Gerard Houllier.

Houllier, recently appointed coach of French champions Lyon, was a close observer of Australia during the recent Confederations Cup in Germany as a member of FIFA's Technical Committee.

Boultbee would neither confirm nor deny Damiano, previously an assistant to Houllier at the French Football Federation and Liverpool, was on the FFA's shopping list.

"Damiano certainly hasn't come across my desk but Gerard Houllier may have mentioned him to someone else," Boultbee said.

FFA insiders confirmed that Chairman Frank Lowy was the driving force behind axing Farina and that the moderately successful performance by the Farina-led Australian under-23 side at the Olympic Games last year saved the axe from falling earlier.

"Frank Lowy has thought Australia has needed a foreign coach since the Olympics in Athens but Farina was saved for a while by the team making the quarter-finals at that tournament," a source said, speaking on condition of anonymity. "There is no doubt whatsoever that Lowy has had a specific shortlist in place prior to Farina's sacking."

Although FFA Chief Executive John O'Neill said earlier this year his coach was safe in his job until the end of Australia's World Cup campaign, Farina had been under intense scrutiny and pressure over the past 12 months. Poor performances against Turkey, Iraq, Indonesia, and New Zealand set alarm bells ringing with the final nail in Farina's coffin being the turgid display against Tunisia in Leipzig last month.

A rumoured player revolt against Farina in Germany never eventuated but team members have responded to the decision to axe Farina in a "businesslike" manner, according to insiders. A source close to Farina said the coach, who had been at the Socceroos helm since 1999, had been battered by events over the past year.

"It was definitely all getting to him," the source said. "It had all seriously worn him down."

HARRY KEWELL PRAYS HE DOESN'T BREAK DOWN

Liverpool, May 2005

Harry Kewell travels to Istanbul with his Liverpool team on Monday having described this week's UEFA Champions League Final as the biggest match of his life. Kewell fought off a season-long groin injury to be fit for Liverpool's showdown against Milan, the historic match adding a rare sprinkle of stardust to the most challenging season of the Socceroo's career. Watched by a worldwide television audience of millions, Kewell now has a major role in the final of the biggest and richest club competition in the world - of any sport.

"This is the biggest game of my life," Kewell said. "If you can't get pumped up for this game then what can you get pumped up for? You want to play, you want to start, and hopefully win. I don't get more nervous than a regular game but it's exciting with the buildup. The past week has been nothing but talk about the Champions League final. It is all good."

Kewell played through pain for the first half of the season with a mystery groin injury before seeking radical physiotherapy treatment from Dutch, German, Spanish, and Australian experts after Liverpool's in-house medical staff were unable to cure him. The injury has frustrated both Kewell and Liverpool boss Rafael Benitez who has been desperate to include the Australian wing wizard in his starting line-up.

"I wouldn't describe the season as up and down, I would say that it's been all down," Kewell said. "I've had this groin injury from the start and it has plagued me all season. You go out there and try your hardest and you just can't do it. Then there are people out there hammering you saying there's nothing wrong with you."

Although still not fully fit, Kewell made a timely return for the Champions League semi-finals against Chelsea last month, coming off the bench in both legs. Excellent results in Europe this season for

Liverpool have come in the face of a disappointing Premier League campaign but the Anfield side is confident the trip to Turkey heralds a return to the club's glory days of the 1970s. Liverpool last played in the final of Europe's top club competition, then named the European Cup, in 1985 when they lost 1-0 to Juventus.

That match was marred by the tragic death of Juventus fans in what became known as the Heysel disaster and led to English clubs being banned by governing body UEFA from competing in Europe for five years. This season Liverpool are underdogs but have stunned observers by beating heavyweights Chelsea, Juventus, Bayer Leverkusen, and Monaco on the route to Istanbul.

"Every team is only human," Kewell said. "Rafael Benitez has worked the other teams out really well and how to play against them. That's how we got to the final. We're the first to hold our hands up to our inconsistencies in the league. We know we can do better. But Europe is a different ball game, literally. You play teams from different countries, different situations, away goals to consider. There is a lot more going on. The boss knows how to play against certain teams and we're going to go out against Milan and do our job. If we can perform to how we played against Chelsea, Juventus, and Olympiakos, then it would be fantastic and we will have a great chance."

Kewell acknowledged the criticism he had received from the media in the UK and Australia for failing to recover from his injuries. With medical staff unable to pinpoint the issue that has plagued him all season it had been a battle to regain total fitness."

"I know that shouldn't affect me but it is annoying when people assume things when they don't even talk to me," he said. "They should get the facts first then make their mind up. When they are shouting things willy-nilly, they sound stupid. Everyone is allowed their opinion but these people are ridiculous. Anyone can comment on anyone without knowing the facts. They are wrong. They look like idiots."

"One day it feels fine and the next I can't walk. The next day it starts to get better again and the next I can't walk again. The next day it feels great. It messes with my mind. The last thing I want to do is have an operation but I have tried everything. I'm just going to keep working on it and see where it takes me. I am working day and night, 24-7 on this, and if I can be 100 percent for the final, I will be there. I am going to give it my all to be there."

"I am praying I don't break down."

Postscript: Kewell started the game and was substituted in the 23rd minute after tearing his adductor muscle.

GUUS HIDDINK WITH WIND IN HIS HAIR

Sydney, July 2005

Guus Hiddink was introduced to the Australian media at the Westfield organization's headquarters in Sydney at the end of July. Frank Lowy had delivered with his replacement for Frank Farina. There was no contest. The love affair between Australia and Hiddink began in that room. Things were serious. After a press conference, I was ushered into a side room to speak to the Dutchman. Noted: he asked almost as many questions about Australia as I asked him about his career and football philosophy. It was a conversation about football unlike any with an Australian coach.

"We have to arm ourselves mentally and strategically," he said. "We must also be honest and realistic. It will be very difficult but, in the short time we have, we hope to prepare a team that's very competitive but can also adapt to the circumstances in South America."

The 58-year-old Dutchman, who will coach PSV Eindhoven concurrent with the Socceroo job, said he plans for Australia to use a style of play he has employed previously with Valencia, Holland, South Korea, and PSV.

"It is total football," he said. "It is about flexibility in all positions. In modern football, technical skill must be OK but physical skill, mobility, and pace must be on a good level. You must be a good athlete just to survive. I don't separate the defensive or attacking parts of the team. This is what total football is about. My concept is to play for two moments: when we have possession of the ball and when we don't."

Hiddink opened the door for comebacks to the national team for veterans Paul Okon and Ned Zelic - both discarded under former coach Frank Farina - saying players would be judged on current performance not history.

"It's too early for me to say specifically [whether Paul Okon or Ned Zelic will be recalled]," Hiddink said. "The only thing that counts, whether the players are 19 or 34, is their performance and who is playing in a specific position."

Hiddink' CV was impeccable. He could list Spanish sides Real Madrid, Real Betis and Turkish giants Fenerbahce as former club and said he was familiar with Australia's high-profile players, especially those in the English Premier League.

However he acknowledged he will call on technical manager Ron Smith and assistant coach Graham Arnold for specialised advice on Australian talent.

"I'm talking to the staff about players who have not been involved recently," Hiddink said. "I don't count the past much. I'm not going to ask why some players have not been chosen."

Hiddink said Australia's sieve-like defence - the Socceroos conceded 10 goals at the Confederations Cup - will be a priority in his planned makeover of the national team.

"Of course, when you get 10 goals that is 10 too many," he said. "Ten is a lot of goals to concede and we have to analyse that. I have seen the games from the Confederations Cup many times on DVD and I'm working out how to solve that problem."

Hiddink is known in Holland for attention to detail but is relaxed in his relationship with players. He enjoys an occasional beer and spends spare time riding a Harley Davidson motorbike - a trait he shares with Australia's now reclusive 1974 World Cup captain, Peter Wilson.

"I go for a ride every now and then especially when it's sunny weather," Hiddink said. "I like to ride to freshen my mind. I've been riding for about 10 years but I don't like bikes that go very fast. I like to enjoy nature and the wind in my hair."

Hiddink was mobbed by Korean tourists at the Opera House on Friday. His visit to Sydney, his first ever trip to Australia, ends on Sunday night when he returns to Holland and immediate duty with PSV Eindhoven.

"This is all very exciting for me," he said.

WIDE AWAKE IN MARRAKECH

Marrakech, September 2005

"Thank you and enjoy your dessert," said Youssou N'Dour, the Senegalese music star as he ended his performance at FIFA's 55th congress in Marrakech. N'Dour was the musical entertainment during the "gala dinner", an opportunity to hit the trough with 600 people from every country on Earth (except Yemen, suspended, and Libya, who got lost on the way, apparently).

The evening amply demonstrated just how surreal life with FIFA could be. If eating a five-course fish dinner in the middle of the Moroccan desert is not strange enough, perhaps 200 catering staff being flown in from Germany for the night might tip things over the edge. FIFA President Sepp Blatter once claimed "the future is feminine" but out of about 600 guests, fewer than 50 were women and most of them the wives of VIPs.

Although there were hundreds and hundreds of other dinner guests and no set seating except for the Very Important VIP guests, I sat at an eight-place table with just Les Murray, the SBS-TV icon, as my dinner partner.

"Can you just leave the bottle on the table?" Murray half-asked but more demanded of the German waitress who was looking after our table. The sun was setting over North Africa as she explained that, no, in fact, she couldn't leave a bottle of wine on the table. Dinner protocol required she refill glasses. No bottles on the table.

Murray and I were the only Australian media representatives in Marrakech. I'd run into him at Dubai airport after flying overnight from Melbourne. He was sitting alone in a smoky fake Irish pub, drinking and smoking cigarettes. He looked like he missed Johnny Warren, his longtime partner in crime who had died a year earlier. I turned down his offer of a beer - my body clock told me it was 6am - and told him I would see him at the gate for our flight to Morocco. The Asian Football Confederation had chartered a plane and was flying its delegation – and media – to Marrakech.

Every morning in Morocco, Les Murray would call my room and tell me to meet him by the pool. He would never swim. He sat at a table with a drink and a pack of cigarettes and would tell war stories (not from actual wars) and dissect what he'd heard from the chatter from FIFA delegates around the hotel. I tried to swim laps but mostly listened as he talked about his trips to Asia, Brazil, and the Pacific where he was Australia's representative on a regional television association.

Our conversations continued at our lonely table during the grand dinner and afterwards where, after the dinner, buses shuttled us back to the hotel where delegates drank at the bar and talked to prostitutes. I passed out on a poolside lounge chair from a combination of jet lag and too much wine mid-conversation with another journalist and an AFC executive. The AFC executive later told me she had draped a blanket over me while I was asleep.

The morning after the dinner (I apparently made it back to my room), delegates from all FIFA's national associations (except the aforementioned absentees) gathered for football's equivalent of parliament. Speeches were made and votes taken on issues of the day. FIFA has been in existence for over 100 years yet this was the first congress on African soil.

"Don't let it be another 100," grumped Issa Hayatou, Sepp Blatter's long-time rival, as the FIFA president made his opening address. Africa may have been celebrated but much side discussion focused on Asia. AFC president Mohamed Bin Hammam, was being touted as a serious candidate to succeed Blatter and was keen to highlight what he considered the foreign imperialisation of Asian football.

The Premier League permeated some Asian countries deeply. Singapore's national league played fixtures midweek to avoid clashes with satellite TV coverage of English games. "Imagine in England that a Brazilian club, or even a French or Italian one, comes in and has a hold on English football," Bin Hammam told me the day after we arrived as we sat in the courtyard of the hotel the AFC had commandeered.

"In England, they put their own football first." Both Bin Hammam and Blatter rounded on Asian pre-season tours by European clubs. The perception in Asia is that the clubs come for nothing but the money. And then run.

"Your market should not accept it," Blatter told a gathering of Asian journalists. "Those tours are a circus. The clubs go there to take your money. Some go east to Asia; some go west to the United States. Then, when the players get called for their national teams, the clubs say they are tired!"

Speaking of a circus, the preparation for the media meeting with Blatter gave an insight into how Asian media worked from a different perspective than what were the norms for Australia at the time. The journalists were called to a pre-interview meeting with an AFC representative to discuss who would provide the welcoming address to Blatter, who would ask what questions, and what those questions would be.

"We've got about 10 minutes with this guy, just get some good questions to him," I suggested, frustrated. This was the first time Australian media (ie, me and Murray) engaged with the AFC since joining the confederation. Most of our new colleagues were aghast at the suggestion to quickly cut to the point. Les Murray took me aside.

"You have to remember that many of these people are from places where the media toes the party line and it's not the done thing to be direct to people in authority," he suggested.

"Yeah, but we're not from those places," I replied, "and Blatter and Bin Hammam know that."

Bin Hammam's not outrageous plan was to build ten sustainable leagues across Asia that would – eventually – rival Europe, for both fans and players in their prime. This was 2005 but he was thinking long-term.

"I want one day for players like Ronaldinho, Ronaldo, Henry,

Zinedine Zidane, to see that there are opportunities for them to play in Asia and earn as good as they can in Europe," he said.

"In the future, economically, Asia can be number one. My dream is for Asia to compete in attracting the top stars of the world. This is where we can make Asia on the level of Europe or at least next to Europe. It can be achieved and not just in Japan, Korea and Australia, for example. There is a lot of potential for the leagues to be developed in India and China, the big two potential markets, and the Middle East."

Two nights earlier (it always seemed like it was night in Marrakech), in a tent constructed in another luxury hotel in the city a Slovakian-born Australian jew presented a Qatari Arab with a flag bearing the Southern Cross and a Union Jack. Frank Lowy and Bin Hammam (for it was they) hugged, kissed, and referred to each other as friends and brothers.

Football Federation Australia, and its chairman Lowy, was being officially welcomed by Bin Hammam, as a member of the AFC. Delegates from 46 AFC nations, from Lebanon to Uzbekistan and East Timor, waved green cards in the air approving Australia's entry into Asia. FIFA president Sepp Blatter and his predecessor, the corrupt Brazilian Joao Havelange, were in the tent and clapped approvingly.

"They are not Green Cards immigration to the USA," an official hosting proceedings joked. But for Australian football they provide as much opportunity. Prime Minister John Howard has realised the value of the Socceroos new presence in Asia and sent a video message to the ceremony.

"We are very proud with our involvement with the Football Federation of Asia [sic]," he said, turning away from his beloved cricket for 30 seconds. "The government very strongly supports the growth and expansion of the game throughout Australia. We share the enthusiasm and commitment to the game as the followers of soccer, not only at a grass roots level but at the more elite level."

Howard never misses an opportunity. Football provides a platform that no other sport can for Australian foreign policy and business across Asia and around the world. Lowy has delivered a potentially big gift to Howard's government.

"I am very emotional today," he said to Bin Hammam. "I thank you from the bottom of my heart that you are taking us in to the AFC. I have been a football fan since I was a little boy when I went with my father to games. I have been working very hard for the day when I can realise some of the dreams I have had for Australia."

Bin Hammam, it would be revealed in years to come, was terribly and deeply flawed but was sharp. On the return flight from Marrakech to Dubai, he sat in economy class with his two daughters and AFC staff rather than up front with VIP delegates – even though seats were spare in business and first class. He was also aware of the subtle economic shift taking place within global football, pointing out that half of the big-money official sponsors of the 2006 World Cup – Hyundai, Sony and Emirates – are from Asian countries. "Asia is very different now even from 2002," he said. "Today, the world needs us. They need our sponsors. They need our TV audiences."

England strongly fancied its chances to host the 2018 World Cup (in 2005 Blatter had gone so far as to welcome talk of such a bid and Russia was not yet officially on the radar) but even in 2005 Bin Hammam thought an AFC nation would provide the greatest rival. Sepp Blatter revealed the rotational system for World Cup hosting right will be dropped for 2018, allowing cross-continental rivalries to hit fever pitch.

"The rotation system only goes until 2014," Blatter said. "It was a political decision to ensure the World Cup went to Africa, otherwise Africa would never have it."

"There will be good contenders for 2018," he added. "China will definitely make a bid because if they organise the Olympics then they will want the World Cup, but there is the same to be said for Australia. If I am still alive in 2018, I will be retired, and I look forward to watching the games in a famous stadium, maybe in Beijing or maybe Sydney."

If we knew then what we know now. We flew back to Dubai

on another AFC chartered plane. It was slow getting off the plane. Bin Hammam stood at the door - the way flight attendants wave goodbye - but kissed every exiting passenger on both cheeks. Within five years, Asia and Qatar would have the 2022 World Cup. Within 10 years, Bin Hammam and Blatter would be disgraced and Les Murray would soon be dead, taking many stories he rarely told with him.

MONTEVIDEO DIARY: "GOODBYE, GOOD LUCK, AND WELL PLAYED."

Montevideo, November 2005

Thursday, Buenos Aires

When the ball hits the back of the net for the first goal, La Bombonera goes off big time. The Chocolate Box, Boca Juniors home ground, is stuffed with 57,000 rabid fans screaming, shouting, who had been pleading for Boca to pull back an early goal.

The Buenos Aires side, which has produced some of Argentina's greatest players, including Diego Maradona, is locked in a tense battle with Internacional, from Brazil, in a quarter-final of the Copa Sudamericana, a knockout tournament for clubs across South America. Boca have had to overcome a 1-0 deficit from the first-leg.

Across from our seats (actually concrete slabs high above a corner flag) sit Diego Maradona and his guest, Guus Hiddink. Within hours of Australia's arrival in Buenos Aires, Maradona called Hiddink to anoint Australia as victors against Uruguay. As you do. And with God on Australia's side, anything may be possible.

Maradona is everywhere in Buenos Aires. A few nights before the Boca match, we watched, open mouthed, La Noche Del 10 ("The Night of the 10"), Maradona's extravagant TV variety show. There is no Australian comparison. But if Harry Kewell were to host a revived Hey Hey It's Saturday, dressed head to toe in a white suit surrounded by pom-pom waving cheerleaders, you would be one-quarter there. Add Mark Bosnich playing the role of Red Symons (in Maradona's case, former Argentina goalkeeper Sergio Goycocheya) and you begin to get a clearer idea. Add guests – in this case Mike Tyson – and you have a show unlike many others.

Boca beat Internacional 4-1 in a pulsating game. A section of the Boca fans is known as La Doce, or "The 12th". To the team, the feverish support is the extra player on the pitch. Among the visiting

Aussies, it's decided that level of support will be required back in Sydney. Little did we know...

Friday, Montevideo

Our arrival in Montevideo, a few hours ahead of the team, is so low key we may have arrived in Ballarat rather than the assumed seething cauldron of fiery hate that many had expected. There was no violence at the airport as there was four years ago. Then, thugs hired by a marketing company jostled the Australian players in a bid to intimidate them. It worked so well that, this time, Football Federation Australia is given full diplomatic status by the embarrassed Uruguayan government after Australia's embassy in Argentina used a month's worth of shuttle diplomacy across the River Plate to ensure no repeat of 2001.

Some Uruguayan football officials were unrepentant and were privately aghast at what they saw as Australian paranoia over security arrangements. "If we carried on like the Australians have done, we would have been called poofters at home," said one Uruguayan official - off the record.

The biggest danger to any arriving Australians at the airport are the duty-free shop girls dressed up in red coats and tight, tight, white pants (apparently advertising whiskey). Or maybe the group of eight-year-old schoolgirls dressed in red and white checked pinafores.

Later, outside the Radisson Hotel in downtown Montevideo, a group of school kids gather to welcome the Socceroos team bus.

"Mark Viduka is the best in the Australian team," screams Maximilian, who says he's 10 years old. Maybe he's picking a fight. "But Diego Forlan is better."

"Well, Forlan better watch out for Vince Grella," we hit back. "Grella will eat Forlan for breakfast, lunch, and dinner."

The bemused kid doesn't respond, either because we've struck the first dagger into (10-year-old) Uruguayan hearts or he's never heard of Vince Grella. Or he just has no idea what we're talking about.

Late afternoon, the squad heads to the Estadio Centenario to train. Even empty, the stadium is imposing, a concrete bowl with no modern day facilities. We're led underground through cavernous corridors (decorated by posters from past World Cups), past simple dressing rooms, and up onto the pitch.

The Australian team appears calm and confident. Guus Hiddink jokes with the media. The sun sets across the stadium. After training, Harry Kewell reveals the confidence Hiddink has given the team. "We're only contemplating winning," he says.

Saturday, Game Day

The booing and whistling began when Mark Schwarzer came out to warm up with goalkeeping coach Tony Franken. It continued when the rest of the team appeared and went on when the first bars of Advance Australia Fair chimed. By accident or design, Australia's national anthem begins before the teams even line up. Advance Australia Fair is obliterated by crowd noise but the stadium falls silent for The Fatherland or Death, Uruguay's national anthem. The entire 65,000 stadium (minus 100 Australians) sings along (sample lyric: "Let tyrants tremble, our country or the grave").

Despite the booing, Uruguay is perhaps the only country in the world where its football team is in no way a reflection of its people. With Richard Morales and his mates as ambassadors, the impression could quickly be formed that Uruguay is a country of rabid kangaroo hunters baying for Aussie blood. The streets? Desperately unsafe. The people? Rude and inhospitable to anyone wearing green and gold.

The reality is so far the opposite.

"Meet my new Australian mates," a taxi driver shouts to a colleague at a set of traffic lights. He lets us hang a Southern Cross flag out of his window and honks his horn at Uruguayan fans. Who wave back.

,"Don't talk to me about Alvaro Recoba," says Juan, at the hotel after the match. Many Uruguayans realise 1-0 is not enough to take to Sydney.

"You guys were great," says the waiter at a neighbourhood restaurant (we eat at midnight after the game – the restaurant is still full). "Who do you think will go to Germany?"

"Australia," we answer. "Possibly."

"You're probably right," he answers. "So good luck."

The best advertisement for the real Uruguay occurs when the Australian team leaves the Estadio Centenario after the game. The exit is deserted, except for bored riot police, wanting to go home and watch a replay of the game on TV, and a collection of Uruguayan fans. Among the fans are three generations of one family. A grandmother, a mother and father, and two young kids. They hold a Uruguayan flag as the Australian bus pulls away.

"Goodbye, good luck, well played," they shout in Spanish. "Thank you, have a safe trip."

Tony Popovic, on the top deck of the bus, smiles and waves back.

Sunday, The Day After

Montevideo's streets are deserted. Locals are either at family lunches or local parks playing football. One game takes place in the Ciudad Viejo, the old town now a residential ghetto among empty derelict warehouses. Players, old and young, kick a ball in the afternoon sun across a dirt pitch. The ball is regularly lost in a storm of dust or under passing buses as teams play with as much intensity, if not talent, as Vince Grella, Harry Kewell, and Alvaro Recoba had the day before. A man walks up the touchline offering lollies for a peso, less than five cents, to friends and families watching the game.

"Hey, Australianos!" calls out one man, noticing strangers among the crowd. "Well played yesterday, huh? A great game, yes? Good luck!"

Everyone seems to wish luck to everybody in Montevideo.

Wednesday, Game Two

At 6.30am, Montevideo appears quiet, even if cafés and bars are full of fans attempting to get the best position in front of TVs. If, as Australians, we're nervous watching the biggest event in recent Australian sports history behind enemy lines then the locals are more so. Few people are talking. We order breakfast but can't eat. A cup of coffee is sculled. Maths: is drinking scotch at 7am OK if it's 8pm in Sydney?

When Mark Bresciano scores, our small table is turned into La Bombonera. Our cover is blown. There are Australians in the midst. Expecting a barrage of abuse, all we get is a hello nod and polite applause. The game unfolds. The substitution of Recoba is greeted by groans. Montero's departure by moans. Extra time calls for privacy. We sprint back to the hotel but not before the waiter gives a thumbs up.

"Australia deserves to win," he says.

"But first I think I will be sick," I reply. Later, it occurs that he probably thinks I was commenting on his food rather than my nerves.

The streets are empty for the penalty shootout except for scheduled buses keeping to their timetables. You could feel the country groan when Dario Rodriguez missed his kick. Silence was broken when John Aloisi scored: perhaps the only Australians left in Uruguay let out a roar that, if you were in Sydney, you would have heard had you all not been going nuts yourself.

Two hours later, exhausted, we hailed a cab.

"Where to?" said the driver.

"We're going to Germany," we replied.

"Ah, Australians!" he replied.

He drove straight to the airport without asking if we were taking a plane. And gave us a half-price discount on the fare.

FALLEN AND FORLORN, HARRY KEWELL RISES AGAIN

Montevideo, November 2005

Harry Kewell will walk out in front of a sell-out Telstra Stadium on Wednesday night hoping his hometown crowd will watch him end 12 months of professional hell. Kewell has fought back from a career-threatening injury, including two operations in the past six months, to be fit to play a major role in Australia's bid for World Cup qualification.

Kewell's hunger for Sydney victory comes from being starved of a meaningful role in what could have been a career high. The Australian painfully limped out of Liverpool's UEFA Champions League final against AC Milan in Istanbul last May after just 20 minutes. Two hours later, Liverpool had dramatically fought back from a 3-0 deficit to win the match but without Kewell.

"I wouldn't say it has been a long 12 months, I would say that it has been a dreadful 12 months," Kewell said in Montevideo before boarding a return flight to Australia. "The lowest point was definitely May 25th. The Champions League Final. Walking off the pitch. I was up for the game. I was feeling good. I thought I was fighting fit but as soon as I stuck my leg out my whole adductor snapped. I felt it go and I looked down and I saw a big lump down there. I couldn't move. To be on the biggest stage for club football in the world and to have to come off after 20 minutes was horrible."

Boos from disgruntled Liverpool fans, frustrated at their star midfielder's fitness failures, embarrassingly rang out around the stadium. The fall from grace was magnified by the image of a forlorn and fallen Kewell relayed around the world by international TV coverage.

"I couldn't really hear the booing," Kewell said. "I went out there to do a job and if people were doing that, then each to their own. Everyone has their own opinion but if they knew the true facts about the injury then maybe they would think twice about it. People can say what they like about me. It doesn't bother me. My family and friends were brilliant while I was injured. My wife has been fantastic because she has been the one who has had to deal with me for the last year and a bit. The manager at Liverpool, Rafael Benitez, has been brilliant too. To show confidence in me, by starting me in the Champions League Final, when everyone was turning around and saying, 'What are you doing?', showed great confidence. I really respect that and I need to repay him."

Kewell arrives in Sydney on Monday night for a 72 hour visit that he hopes will change his, and Australian football's, recent history. He believes Sydney has a major role to play in the Socceroos destiny, breaking free of a Melbourne hoodoo after failures at the MCG in 1997 and 2001.

"It will be a big boost playing the last leg in Sydney, not just for the whole Australian team but especially for the Sydney boys," Kewell said. "We have not played a World Cup play-off in Sydney in a long while. Wednesday is going to be something special. Qualification would mean a lot. I want to have played in at least one World Cup before I retire. Many of my friends have been to a World Cup and they say that there is nothing else like it. To be part of that would be something special. We talk about the World Cup when we're with our clubs and it's every footballer's dream to play at one. Every four years the world stops and just watches football."

According to Kewell, Australia's secret weapon may prove to be coach Guus Hiddink. Hiddink's CV includes stints at Réal Madrid and Valencia as well as leading his native Holland to the World Cup in 1998 and South Korea in 2002.

"The difference between Guus and Frank Farina is that Guus has been there and done it while Frank was just starting out in coaching when he took over Australia," Kewell said. "If Frank had got his chance to go to a World Cup four years ago it may have been a different story but things didn't work out like that. Frank is still a big fan of ours and he still wants us to win which is great."

Kewell said his team mates were focused on Wednesday's second leg. Winning the tie on penalties has been considered but losing the tie has not.

"We have not thought about losing," Kewell said. "We have not contemplated it. The players only think about winning."

Penalties? Would Kewell volunteer to take the first, second, or possibly crucial fifth spot-kick?

"It doesn't matter. I am there. Whatever. I think I will have to fight a few people first to get in the line. We have a lot of confident boys in our squad. We will not be too short of players wanting to take them. We have to have, not just 11 men on the park, but the entire squad need to be generals on Wednesday and look after each other. This has to be a real team effort."

"THERE'S NO CHOICE, I'LL BE THE HERO."

Sydney, November 2005

John Aloisi stepped up to take his now famous shootout spot-kick aware that, never mind his football career, the next touch of the ball could define his whole life. The striker had watched from the halfway line as Mark Viduka scuffed his own kick before goalkeeper Mark Schwarzer put Australia in the qualification box seat with his second save. The 29-year-old had entered the fray in added time, a substitute for Mark Bresciano, but knew the time had come to enter his name into Australia's sporting history.

"I was really calm and confident," Aloisi said at home in Vittoria, Spain, in his first interview since the match. "I had the feeling everything was going to turn out for good. We went to the bench and when [assistant coach Graham Arnold] asked who was confident I put up my hand straight away."

"Arnie wanted to put me down as first but I said I wanted to take number five. I had it in my head that I was going to be either the hero or the villain. I didn't know who was going to take the other penalties. I was standing at the halfway line when Harry went up to take his and asked Lucas [Neill] if he was taking one. He then asked me what number I was. I said last."

"I'll be either the hero or the villain," Aloisi told Neill.

"But which will it be?" Neill asked.

"There's no choice," Aloisi replied. "I'll be the hero."

Aloisi admitted to nerves when Mark Viduka skewed his spot kick wide but was buoyed by Mark Schwarzer's second save.

"I think I was the only person in the stadium who didn't jump up, though." he said. "I just began to walk towards the ball thinking 'This is it, this is the penalty to take us to the World Cup'. It was excitement more than nerves. I thought the walk would be a lot more nerve-racking than it was. I was thinking my legs would go and that I'd be so scared but I was confident and happy I was the one who was going to take the penalty that would take us to Germany. Everything was just concentrated on my run up and how I was going to hit it. I didn't even hear the crowd at all. But I certainly heard them when I scored."

Aloisi, who plays for Alaves in Spain, took three days off in hometown Adelaide before returning to Europe. The short break allowed the weight of his spot kick to sink in.

"The day after the game I said to my brother, 'Can you believe if I'd missed and Australia didn't go to the World Cup? I'd never be able to live that down. Don't just worry about my career. It would be there for my whole life afterwards. Those 32 years [since 1974] would be 36 years and then who knows how long after that."

"During the game, I didn't think of the $8 million [Australia received for qualification], or the 20 million Australians in the country, or the 85,000 that were in the stadium," he said. "But afterwards, it started to hit me. Every time I turned on the TV there was something about the Socceroos and people celebrating on the street. I think I've seen my goal about 150 million times now."

"Then I got embarrassed watching my celebration. I keep asking myself why I took my shirt off and everyone has been saying that they've never seen me run so fast. I was running to where my family was sitting and I didn't want to get stopped before I got there."

In the immediate aftermath, Aloisi's wife Angela received congratulatory text messages from the wife of Pablo Garcia, the Uruguay and Réal Madrid midfielder, who had just lost the match. Aloisi also received a message from Javier Aguirre, who took Mexico to the 2002 World Cup, and coached Aloisi, Garcia, and Uruguay bad boy Richard Morales at Osasuna. Beyond his dramatic goal, a lasting image of Aloisi after the match is his post-game exchange with Morales.

"I wished him all the best and said I was sorry," Aloisi said. "One of the first things I thought of was my ex-club teammates. I knew how they must have felt because I've been through it twice before. Morales is an aggressive player but that's just his way of playing. He is a great guy to have on your team. You know that if there's a fight on then you can hide behind him. You have to remember a lot of Uruguayan people come from very poor backgrounds and to get a better life they have to make it in football. It is do or die for them."

Mark Schwarzer arrived at his family home in England on the Saturday after the midweek game in Sydney still shocked by the Australian public's reaction to World Cup qualification. Schwarzer, who made two dramatic saves in Wednesday night's penalty shootout, took a 24-hour flight from Sydney to London on Thursday but could have made the same trip surfing a wave of jubilation. The goalkeeper has barely slept since Wednesday's historic scenes but said, even with little sleep, he has been living the past few days as a dream.

"I've been amazed by how many people the game has affected," Schwarzer said. "People from all over the place have responded and I've only just realised how many people were watching. Qualifying has been a massive boost for the game in Australia and football can unite the country. People have told me that they can't remember feeling like this since Australia won the America's Cup. It's been absolutely enormous. A lot of us thought that, if we did it, qualifying would really affect the country but to actually do it and see the effects is amazing."

Schwarzer and John Aloisi, who scored the match-winning penalty, will not only be remembered for their individual efforts from Wednesday night but also for celebratory sprints to rival Cathy Freeman, the last Australian to set Homebush alight.

"I don't think many people had ever seen me run that fast and I certainly don't think I've run that fast before," Schwarzer said. "I had to slow down and stop so people could catch me. There was a big build up of emotion and adrenaline running through everyone and I was no different to anyone else. I think everyone in the whole stadium would have been doing the same run if they could have got onto the pitch."

The 2006 World Cup campaign is the 33-year-old's third-time lucky. Schwarzer made his international debut for the Socceroos in 1993 as a 20-year-old rookie in a World Cup play-off against Canada. In the return match in Sydney, he saved two penalties in a shoot-out that allowed Australia to face off against Argentina in yet another sudden-death decider against South American opposition. Schwarzer was ignored by Terry Venables in 1997 after a club versus country bust-up but made the number one shirt his own under Frank Farina in 2001.

"The hype will die down a little bit but the momentum will keep going," Schwarzer said of Australian football's new profile. "What the win has done is really put football on the map in Australia. Over the years, the past campaigns, there has been hype about the various teams and various games but it has always been a disappointment in the end. Finally, we had all that hype, all that attention, and we have come through with the goods. This ending was something different for the country and the sport."

Schwarzer said he did not see qualification for next year's World Cup as a declaration of war on other Australian sports. Instead, the occasion was a chance for Australia to celebrate together.

"I am amazed at the number of people from different [football] codes who came up to us and said, 'I am normally a union supporter but I went to the game and I am hooked, it was unbelievable'," Schwarzer said. "There were a couple of rugby league players who came back to our hotel afterwards who were totally absorbed by the whole occasion."

"[The European-based players] live in a part of the world where football is everything. In Australia we are blessed with so many good sporting teams that football has been down the pecking order. It is a little bit different for us right now because we're not used to having football as the number one sport."

Schwarzer said the team were looking forward to next month's World Cup draw that will decide who Australia's initial three opponents will be.

"One thing is getting to Germany and the other is being competitive and making a real go of it, which I am sure we'll do," Schwarzer said. "We are obviously going to be drawn against a very powerful nation, without a doubt. That is one of the difficulties of not being a seeded team. I am not particularly bothered by who we are up against. People talk about fairytales and a rivalry between us and England but I'm not bothered. Personally, I think it would be great if we were in another group to England and we went further and they didn't. That too would be fantastic."

ANDREW JENNINGS WAS RIGHT ABOUT EVERYTHING

Zurich, May 2006

Australia caught a heavy dose of World Cup fever as the Socceroos prepared for Germany in Melbourne during the week. Yet among the hopes, dreams, and ambitions of the Australian team and its supporters – as well as the 31 other competing nations – grey clouds fringe the upcoming tournament. Allegations of bribes, vote rigging, and ticket scandals threaten to rain on FIFA's parade, specifically for Sepp Blatter, the Swiss president of the world governing body.

The smoking gun is an alleged kickback intended for a senior FIFA official that was accidentally sent to FIFA's bank account. The payment, from the now-collapsed International Sport and Leisure marketing company, is subject to investigation from Swiss authorities. According to investigative journalist Andrew Jennings, in a new book Foul!, the payment could expose some of FIFA's top brass to criminal charges.

ISL, responsible for selling hugely lucrative World Cup TV rights around the world, went bust in 2002 still owing FIFA at least US$22 million it had not passed on from a TV deal with a Brazilian network. In 1998, the world governing body received a 1 million Swiss Franc deposit in its account, intended as a secret payment to a top FIFA official who had assisted ISL in winning its contract. Instead of reporting the payment to FIFA's Executive or Finance Committees, Sepp Blatter, then FIFA General Secretary, forwarded the payment to its intended recipient. It has taken eight years for details of the payment to come to light.

"Whether Blatter has taken bribes or not, the people around him have," Jennings said. "The question to Mr Blatter is, what has he done to discover the names of the people who have taken bribes? But Blatter can't answer that question. He could easily find out by going to see the ISL liquidator [who has the evidence] but he hasn't done it.

He should do, and could do, to find out who the bad guys are in his organisation. Name and shame them."

Unsurprisingly, FIFA and Blatter think little of the allegations from Jennings, who previously revealed corruption within the International Olympic Committee in best-selling books The Lords of the Rings and The New Lords of the Rings. Blatter and FIFA threatened Jennings with legal action but the journalist has yet to see the inside of a court on the issue.

Instead, FIFA attempted to ban the book, which also alleges senior FIFA officials have been involved in black market ticket scandals and paid bribes during FIFA elections to ensure they received votes. In a somewhat bizarre move, a judge initially banned Foul! from sale in Switzerland before FIFA withdrew the request.

"Having got it banned, Blatter then realized that he had a legal fight," Jennings said.

FIFA has declared Jennings "persona non grata" and maintains Foul! warrants neither a yellow nor red card for President Sepp Blatter.

"Although the book does contain various defamatory passages and many inaccurate statements and aspersions, this toned-down version of the book makes it unnecessary for FIFA to continue pursuing legal action," said the governing body in a statement.

"They have threatened to sue but never have," Jennings said. "My publishers had five lawyers for nine months climbing all over this book. They basically said that they didn't believe a word of it and I had to prove everything again."

Positions within FIFA can be highly coveted. Executive Committee members have five-star travel expenses paid for and can claim up to US$500 per day allowance while away from home. This is all on top of a US$100,000 annual tax-free salary. If that isn't enough, FIFA vice-president Jack Warner, from Trinidad & Tobago, was the owner of a travel company that obtained exclusive rights to sell tickets to Soca Warrior fans wanting tickets to the World Cup.

A hypothetical Australian equivalent might be Socceroo fans only being able to purchase World Cup packages though a company owned by FFA CEO John O'Neill. The Trinidad scam, where Warner's company received 1,774 tickets from T&T's 10,749 official allocation, was against FIFA rules, according to FIFA's Ethics Committee, a body that includes SBS-TV personality Les Murray on its panel.

Warner fronted the committee in February and was found to have breached the ethics code on six counts. An aghast Ethics Committee, which has no disciplinary power, passed the matter to FIFA's Executive Committee which took no action against Warner, one of its own highest-ranking officials, on the grounds that he had sold his share of the company.

But why should ordinary supporters care?

"Fans have been misled." Jennings said. "Their passion has been stolen."

Jennings adds that complex FIFA politics means it is difficult for national associations to police the organisation. While FIFA has dissidents, Blatter is ruthless with those who do not support him. In 2002, after his controversial re-election, Blatter axed General-Secretary Michel Zen-Ruffinen who was concerned about a perceived lack of transparency and conflicts of interest.

"Can you see the Australian federation asking for an investigation into bribes?" Jennings said. "No. Will the English do it? No. If you offend Blatter you will not get on. There will come a time in Australia though when people ask, what are we getting back and do we support Blatter? Maybe there is a good Australian for the job. So long as they are honest and reasonably organised, they can do they job."

As in Australia, just three years ago when the federal government pushed for reform in the local administration, there is little likelihood of turkeys voting for Christmas. However, a Swiss magistrate may hold a piece of paper that could cause concern for Blatter. Investigating magistrate Thomas Hildbrand has indicted ISL's bosses for embezzling the 1998 Brazilian TV rights money it failed to pay FIFA. After acquiring more information during the ISL investigation,

Hildbrand raided FIFA's Zurich HQ in November last year.

"Any moment there could be a phone call for Mr Blatter to please come with his lawyers to the magistrate's office," Jennings said. "This is a very serious situation."

NO ONE CAN EAT UNTIL GUUS SAYS SO

Mierlo, May 2006

Australia arrived at its Dutch training base near Eindhoven yesterday afternoon for a week of intense World Cup preparation. The Socceroos will be based at the Carlton De Brug ("The Bridge") hotel in the village of Mierlo before shifting base to Rotterdam on Friday ahead of next Sunday's friendly match with Holland. De Brug is a football-friendly hotel 30 minutes drive from the centre of Eindhoven. Tucked away behind a canal and tree-lined suburban streets, the 149-room hotel doubles as the largest conference facility in Europe. Football teams from Europe regularly use the facility as a training camp, making use of purpose-built football fields just 20 steps across a driveway from the hotel's reception.

After a 28-hour flight from Melbourne to Amsterdam, with stopovers in Singapore and London, the team arrived at Mierlo to link up with star player Harry Kewell, who has spent the past week in England recovering from injury. For the next six days, the squad will take a crash course in how to succeed at the World Cup, when Australia play their first game against Japan in Kaiserslautern on June 12. Each day will be divided into morning and afternoon sessions, with at least one workout on the training field scheduled for each day.

Hiddink, along with assistants Graham Arnold and Johan Neeskens, will also sit his team in front of the TV to pour over intimate details of Australia's opponents. Team technical manager Ron Smith has assembled DVD footage on the Japanese, Brazilian, and Croatian teams so that players know as much as possible about the opposition. No stone is left unturned: not just what foot Ronaldinho prefers to kick with (his right) but his preferred food (meat, rice, beans, cooked by his mother).

Last April, Hiddink called the squad members who played

against Uruguay last November to Mierlo for a reunion camp but put football on the backburner. Credited with great psychological and motivational skills, Hiddink instead took the team ten-pin bowling and organised an intra-squad tennis tournament. Then, Hiddink and coach Graham Arnold took on the squad in a doubles tournament, eventually won by Harry Kewell and Lucas Neill. More non-football activities are planned to keep players fresh and focused.

The squad bunk down two to a room. Brett Emerton shares with former Sydney Olympic team mate Jason Culina, Harry Kewell shares with Lucas Neill while captain Mark Viduka's roommate is close friend Josip Skoko. Viduka is also godfather to Skoko's four-year-old son Luka. The team will eat all meals together in a private room on the second floor of the hotel. Protocol dictates no player can begin eating from a buffet until the entire squad is present and Hiddink has given the nod to start.

Newcomers Michael Beauchamp from the Central Coast Mariners and Sydney FC's Mark Milligan will have to quickly get used to a system of self-imposed fines, adjudicated by the players, for meal time tardiness. The dining room is exclusively for the playing and coaching staff. Visitors, including Football Federation officials, must be invited by Hiddink or Arnold to join the team at meal times. Midfielder Vince Grella, who plays for Parma in Italy's Serie A is considered one of the squad's key members at lunch and dinner. Grella brings a block of Parmesan cheese and Prosciutto – smoked Italian ham – from his local store in in the Italian gourmet capital of Parma to all national team camps.

On Friday, the squad will pack its bags for Rotterdam, an hour drive north of Mierlo, where it will prepare for next Sunday's friendly with Holland. On Monday, the day after the match against Guus Hiddink's homeland, the team will leave on a charter flight for Stuttgart in Germany before heading to its nearby training camp at Oehringen.

DON PARKES AND THE BIRTHDAY PRESENT DREAM

Oehringen, June 2006

There was a birthday party at the Socceroo fans' campsite in Ohrnberg on Wednesday. Don Parkes turned 72 and celebrated drinking an apple juice with Socceroo fans a generation or two, or maybe even three, younger than he.

Parkes, a former ground announcer for the St George-Budapest club in Sydney, turned up in Oehringen's main square late on Tuesday afternoon. Shunning the organised tour groups favoured by many Australian fans, Parkes had travelled to Germany from Woy Woy in New South Wales on his own.

Although no one was able to get Parkes to explain his exact route from the Central Coast to a small town in southern Germany he will jokingly confirm a plane was involved. His 1993-era Socceroo shirt, and a 1960s vintage Australia rosette, may have helped locals along the way provide directions.

Before finding the fan campsite, Parkes spent Tuesday night, the eve of his birthday, on a spare bed in an Oehringen hotel room. Ted Smith, who played football for Australia at the 1956 Olympics, took pity on him and offered to share his room.

"We gave them a few drinks so they both got a good sleep," said Andre Krueger, the German Socceroos fan who took on the role of matchmaker.

Back in Australia, Parkes is a member of his local A-League club, the Central Coast Mariners and is patron of The Marinators, the team's supporter group. Local rivalries were set aside on Parkes' birthday. At the fan campsite, he held court in front of a group of Sydney FC fans, members of The Cove, entertaining all with tales of travelling the world watching the Socceroos, from Canada to New Zealand, and now Germany.

"On many occasions I was the sole Socceroo supporter," Parkes said. "There were the officials. the players, the media and there was me. I was the only one in the group paying my own way. But I never lost faith in Australia. I knew qualification could happen but I never thought it would happen in my time."

Parkes recalls watching an England team beat Australia 17-0 in 1950. He shared a beer back in the day with the journalist who coined the name "Socceroos". Parkes didn't make the 1974 World Cup. He was newly married 32 years ago and had just bought his first family home. Parkes admired Frank Arok, coach of Australia in the 1980s, and approves of the Lowy-led revolution of the game.

Last weekend, he said, he went to bed jet-lagged and dreamt Australia was playing Bristol Rovers, a lower-league English team. There were only nine Australian supporters in the crowd. Rovers won 4-0.

"The Poms in the crowd were yelling out that the bloody Aussies couldn't even kick a ball," Parkes explained.

As he tells it, the dream continued Sunday. Australia were playing in a huge stadium. You maybe know the rest about the game against Japan: a sea of yellow; a huge roar from a massive crowd; two teams enveloped in drama; Australia scored three goals in five minutes; heroes were made.

Parkes awoke and realised the dream was reality.

"Qualifying for the World Cup is not the apex," he said. "It is the beginning. The future of football in Australia is the young ones. For as long as I can, I want to encourage the young people. Coming to Germany has been an eye opener for me."

The Sydney fans sang "Happy Birthday" for Parkes at Ohrnberg. No one realised it but we were watching a changing of the guard. The blokes who supported "soccer" when it was a sport for "sheilas, wogs, and poofters," can move on happy. The use-by date of the naysayers, those who probably still use that term, is also looming very, very, large.

Germany is being overrun with young Australians keenly following the Socceroos. Many of them are like the seven players of Prospect United, a team from Blacktown in Sydney's west, staying at the Ohrnberg campsite.

Aged between 19 and 26, the group quit their jobs in Sydney to come to Germany. The catch: they had no match tickets and watched Australia beat Japan on a big screen outside the stadium at Kaiserslautern, happily drinking beer with locals and Japanese fans.

They slept outside Ticketek offices to successfully get seats for the Uruguay match last November but failed to get World Cup tickets in an FFA ballot earlier this year. They came to Germany anyway. Their families back in Sydney are watching eBay in the hope something comes up before they drive their camper van to Munich for Sunday's game against Brazil.

"My goal in life was to get here and now that I am here, that's it," said Andrew Pace, one of the group. "This is the best time of our lives. We even played soccer on the autobahn. There was a traffic jam and it was banked up so we jumped out, put on our Australia shirts, and played a game in between the traffic."

With just four players remaining back in Blacktown, Prospect United's season is looking bleak. But it's all about the big picture, according to those on international duty.

"The four boys left back home are waiting for us to come back," said Pace. "This season is a write off but we are building for next season. In Prospect, people with prospects want to buy a house but all you need in life is a sleeping bag and tent."

Although a couple of tickets to some Australia games would help, too.

HERR MAISENBACHER'S TEARS ARE ALL OF US

Oehringhen, June 2006

On Wednesday morning, Herr Maisenbacher cried.

The owner, manager and cook of the Pfedelbacher Hof had been a man of few words over the past three weeks but he was never short of emotion. Trudging back into his guesthouse after returning from the Italy game in Kaiserslautern on Monday night, he'd greeted us at his front door. "Schwein!" he said, shaking his head. Pigs! He wasn't reading from his menu but describing what he thought about the Italian team that had just played Australia.

He spoke no English and our German remained restricted to a few items on menus, the word "bier", and the numbers one to 10. So Herr Maisenbacher mimicked a bird and then someone diving. The Italian had swallow-dived, he thought. "Schwein!" he said again.

"Spaghetti? Nicht! Pizza? Nicht!" He was scrubbing Italian items off his menu.

And we thought we were upset.

Herr Maisenbacher, like many of the locals around Oehringen, took Australia's exit hard. One day, the town had been full of Australians, dressed in gold, drinking, laughing, (and spending money). Then, in the aftermath of a poor attempt at a tackle, we were gone. Sudden. Abrupt. Brutal. There was a kind of a death and few people had the chance to say goodbye.

Oehringen had claimed to be Australia's most northern city before the World Cup, a bid to lure fans to visit. It worked but not because of any marketing campaign. Besides being the temporary home of the Socceroos, Oehringen genuinely took the Australians, the team, fans, and media, to heart. Aussie fans were popular during the World Cup and several cities had hoped the Socceroos would play at their stadiums. Australian supporters were fun. They carried inflatable kangaroos. They spent money. They drank and caused no trouble, more likely to fall asleep in the street than want to fight in it.

On Tuesday night, Domenico and his wife Claudia hosted a party at their restaurant for any Australians still left in Oehringen after the defeat. Domenico is from Italy and wore an Italia apron but he was slightly embarrassed about the nature of his team's victory. Claudia, originally from Poland, said "I love you!" to her guests regularly through the night. It was the only English she knew. As well as Australians at the party, there were locals and it was a stellar cast.

There was the man born in Oehringen who had lived there all his life, perhaps bizarrely only leaving once a year to attend Mardi Gras in Sydney. There was Maria, a melancholy Scarlett Johansson look-a-like who, if she did not work at Oehringen's ice-cream shop, had the looks for Hollywood. She wants to study architecture and thinks Melbourne might be a good place to start.

Then there was Ivica, Domenico's head waiter. From Zadar, in Croatia, he supported Hajduk Split. His face lit up when he was shown a text message from former Socceroo Steve Horvat, who once played for Hajduk. Before Australia played Croatia, Ivica said his heart was with the Balkan nation and his big toe for Australia. Returning to Oehringen after the famous 2-2 draw, he had something of a conversion. On Tuesday night, as the party died down, we played football in the town square. Ivica demanded to be in goal. "You're Joe Didulica," we told him, suggesting he pretend to be the Australian-born reserve goalkeeper for the Croatian team. Ivica feigned insult. "No!" he said. "I am Zeljko Kalac!"

The game was eventually broken up at 11.20 by the local police. It was the first and only time they had come to quell Australian - and local - spirits. The potential crime, they said, was that after 11pm you could not play football on the square. For us, the World Cup was over. For Oehringen, the world's biggest sporting event had been on its streets for three weeks - a town that would never otherwise attract much attention. Somewhere that "nothing ever happens", according to Maria, had been, briefly, the centre of a universe.

On Wednesday morning, Herr Maisenbacher gave us a bottle of local red wine and a clumsy hug. Then he burst into tears and so did we. We were gone. So were an extraordinary few weeks.

THE ETERNAL SEARCH FOR THE NEXT BIG THING

Lisbon, August 2006

In Holland last May, before Australia's World Cup campaign kicked off, assistant coach Graham Arnold turned to Kaz Patafta and delivered a wake-up call to the young player's ambition and confidence.

"Arnie said that I wasn't even born when he was trying to get to the World Cup so I shouldn't waste my time here," Patafta recalled.

Guus Hiddink, impressed with potential, had summoned Patafta to train with the Socceroos. The 17-year-old may not have been part of Australian football's chequered past but the plan is that he's very much the future. In Mierlo, where the Australian team prepared for its trip to Germany, Patafta was a welcome sideshow while most observers concentrated on the soap opera that starred Harry Kewell's tender groin.

Patafta impressed in training drills, pulling tricks and ambitious skills out of his kit bag in scratch matches against players who would go on to impress at the World Cup. With Kewell's participation at the tournament in doubt until the last minute, a cruel but recurring question (in Australian football) was asked: is Kaz Patafta the next Harry Kewell? The answer, of course, is no. There really is only one Harry Kewell. But where is Australia's next big thing? Patafta brushes away suggestions he might be Australia's next football idol.

"I look up to Harry so much because he's achieved what I am aiming for myself," Patafta said. "I can also relate to him, being a foreign player, by himself at a big club in Europe. Harry is one of my idols."

There's a catch. While Guus Hiddink rated him, the Australian public has barely heard of Kaz Patafta, if at all, and even though he captained Australia at the World Youth Championship in Peru last year, he was bizarrely unable to earn an A-League contract last season. However, Portuguese giants Benfica saw something no Australian club could and last January Patafta signed with the club that was once home to the legendary Eusebio. It's been a rocket ride over the past nine months. Alongside his Socceroo cameo, the kid from Canberra survived an end-of-season cut at Benfica when 15 friends from the youth team didn't. Last week Patafta was called into the club's first team squad.

"Growing up in Canberra, it was always my dream to play in Europe," Patafta said. "I just wanted it so bad. Unfortunately, I didn't get any offers from A-League clubs. It would have been ideal to get that experience at first team level but the way things have turned out it has been good for me anyway."

Under FIFA regulations, Patafta's father must be in Lisbon with his son and lives in his own apartment while Kaz resides at Benfica's state-of-the-art training facility with the club's other foreign players. Patafta takes Portuguese lessons but is also being schooled in the art of survival. Football in Europe is big business and a door to opportunity. Patafta's rivals are not just players from other teams but kids from Portugal, Mozambique, Brazil, and Angola.

"It is cut throat," Patafta said. "These boys have the same dream as me and the reality is that only one player will step up. On the field it is competitive even though we wear the same jersey. You can't hold back. You can't wait for people. I am not here to make friends. I am here for myself."

Guus Hiddink called another of Australia's next-big-things to Holland: Kristian Sarkies, a midfielder with A-League side Melbourne Victory. Hiddink was impressed enough to consider Sarkies as a last-minute replacement for Kewell and Tim Cahill if Australia's star players did not recover from injury. Yet after the Socceroos training camp broke for Germany, the fates of Patafta and Sarkies split. Patafta is fast-tracked at Benfica while Sarkies now struggles to get a game in the A-League. According to Bernie Mandic, who has been Harry Kewell's manager since the Socceroo was Patafta's age, the lack of player development in Australia is becoming a serious issue.

"Kristian Sarkies is the only player in the A-League that I believe is ready to immediately play in Europe," Mandic said. "What he showed with the Socceroos in Holland was outstanding and the fact Guus left him as cover for Kewell and Cahill demonstrated that Hiddink thinks he is good enough for Europe. But for some reason he has not been able to get a regular start with Melbourne Victory. The same thing happened with Stuart Musialik with Newcastle last season. This sort of nonsense not only damages the player and their confidence but it is also counter-productive for the long-term future of Australian football."

Leo Karis, an agent who represents Central Coast Mariners coach Laurie McKinna, former Australia captain Paul Okon, Michael Beauchamp and recent Socceroos call-up Travis Dodd, is another on the lookout for Australia's next superstar. Karis believes Sarkies and Patafta will take very different paths to the 2010 World Cup, if not just over the next 12 months.

"The difference will be enormous," Karis said. "Kristian will be under pressure to help win matches for a coach who is under enormous pressure this season. Therefore Ernie Merrick's primary focus is to win matches, because his employer demands that, not develop Sarkies, Adrian Leijer, or other young players. This is confirmed by Merrick's obsession with signing Brazilians instead of local players."

"Patafta, on the other hand, will be developed. He will have a technical football system instilled in him where ball control, first touch, vision, and flair will form part of his development."

Mandic states strongly that Harry Kewell's transition from Smithfield superstar to World Cup hero was no accident. Talented Australian kids have long been seduced by the magic of a European contract and European clubs have been fast to flutter eyelids at raw talent.

Marriages are not made in heaven, however, and a brief glance at the playing history of many A-League players show many failed romances with clubs across Europe.

"Harry was not a fluke," Mandic said. "His father Rod was probably the most important difference in how Harry's career has developed. He avoided the trap of being seduced by the promises of fame and fortune from glamorous clubs and opted for Leeds – a club that was

in a rebuilding phase and a club that, at the time, had Britain's best youth development program."

"Unfortunately, most parents fall for the exaggerated promises of agents and clubs and their sons pay the price. I know of at least five other players that had the potential to be in our starting 11 at the World Cup if their parents' egos and greed hadn't led them to opt for clubs that were beyond the players ability. We are constantly fed the nonsense that so-and-so is the next Kewell or Viduka but everyone forgets that our best players were all first-team regulars in Europe by the time they were 20."

According to Karis, unless there is radical overhaul of local coaching systems, there are several possible teenage prodigies who will be forced offshore if they are serious in following Kewell's footsteps. Terry Antonis has been courted by European clubs ever since he was unveiled three years ago as a 10-year-old wonderkid.

"Terry has been courted by European giants for the past two years and is an exceptional talent who will travel to Italy three or four times in the next 12 months for month-long training," Karis said. "If the Australian coaching systems are not overhauled now then Terry has outgrown those Australian systems."

A quick fix for FFA, which is struggling with the introduction of an elite youth league and overhauling youth coaching, will not be easy. But as the A-League kicks off this weekend count the number of young players on the pitch compared with those past their best.

"There is only one logical solution," suggested Mandic. "The FFA should mandate that each A-League team must field at least two under-20 players in any match that the team plays. This way, no team would be at a disadvantage and it would force them to pay more attention to youth development."

Karis believes the search for the next Kewell requires comprehensive overhaul: "With a 20-player roster and just two under-20s included, as A-League rules are now, it is not possible to produce star kids. A youth league is required to develop 150 to 200 players. It also requires expert technical coaching. Imagine what Guus Hiddink could do with a centralized youth policy."

Last week, in Lisbon, Kaz Patafta experienced a 24-hour high and low common to many want-to-be professionals. With a strong contingent of local players trying to break through Benfica's youth system, a foreigner like Patafta can cop many cold shoulders. On this occasion, it was a youth team coach spelling out the reality of success.

"My coach was telling me last week that it was tough here at Benfica and not to get upset if they loan me out to another club," Patafta said. "It was very negative talk."

Ironically, Patafta joined Benfica at a time when it was becoming known for buying players rather than developing its own talent. But the day after the reality check, the same youth team coach received a phone call from the club's new head coach.

"The first team wanted me for a game," Patafta said. "They were all pretty shocked. It hasn't happened in a while that a youth team player has been called up. I am keeping my feet on the ground but it is only impossible if you tell yourself that it is. It is a good feeling to prove people wrong when they don't believe you."

AT HOME AGAINST THE MAFIA, MATCH-FIXING, AND RIOTS

Palermo, September 2006

Fifty people injured, five arrests, eight goals, and a five-star performance: Mark Bresciano's first Sicilian derby was one for the scrapbook. Bresciano starred for new team Palermo as they beat local rivals Catania 5-3 in a game where clashes between rivals fans before and during the match added spice to an already volatile recipe on the pitch.

"For the fans, it was like a war," Bresciano said. "Five people were arrested and 50 were injured. Before the season started everyone was telling me that this was the game of the season, don't worry about the others, this was the result that mattered. You think, yeah, OK, and then the game comes and it's unbelievable. I have never experienced anything like it."

After four years with Parma, Bresciano moved to Palermo following the 2006 World Cup. The club has had a start to its season as bright as its pink shirts. Three games played, three wins, and a town more known for its mafia connections is top of Serie A. Bresciano, too, has benefited: he scored a brilliant bicycle kick on his debut and was credited with a man-of-the-match performance against Catania.

"It makes a change to be in this position," Bresciano said. "I've never had this feeling before and it's great. With Parma, we would always be fighting relegation and struggling from the beginning, so this is a great start for me. It was time to move on from Parma. I had been there for four years. It was good there for the two years before the club hit financial problems but then it was tough. They were bringing in players from the youth team and not signing very many others either. Plus, it was good to know that I'd have my wages in the bank every month.'

Italy, as is now history, won the World Cup in July. Australia, as is now legend, were controversially eliminated by the Azzurri, thanks to that dubiously penalty. A twist to the tale is that prime suspect Fabio Grosso – who was the lead character in the incident that won Italy its last-minute penalty against the Socceroos – was a Palermo player until his own move to Inter after the World Cup.

"I didn't get to meet him," Bresciano said. "He'd gone to Inter by the time I arrived but our two defenders - Cristian Zaccardo and Andrea Barzagli - were in the Italy squad and said that playing Australia was their hardest game of the tournament. People here have said that we fought hard, we were a good team, and that it wasn't a penalty but I guess they can say that now that they won the World Cup. But it did a lot for our reputation. Australia now has respect, especially in Europe, and that is important."

While Fabio Cannavaro lifted the tiny World Cup trophy above his head amid fireworks and streamers, a dark cloud obscured the Azzurri's achievements in Germany. Bresciano said the match-fixing scandal involving several clubs including Juventus and Milan, dampened celebrations.

"People are happy that they won the World Cup but that has been clouded by a lot of the crap that's gone on with the match fixing," Bresciano said. "As a player, you feel cheated. Especially as Parma was involved in a lot of the games involving the teams that were caught out so you have to think what was really going on in some games. But as a player, what can you do? They've punished the clubs hard and that has hurt them and it has hurt the game here. Some players are now saying that they don't want to play in Italy because of all the stuff that went on. It has gone that deep."

GRAHAM ARNOLD AND THE DRAMA QUEENS

Sydney, December 2006

Just this once, Graham Arnold can be allowed to take an easy option. Asked to list his best moment from a year that saw football reach undreamed of heights in Australia, the Socceroo coach didn't hesitate - to name almost every waking hour.

"Personally, nearly every day this year has been a good moment," Arnold said, before unrolling memories from the World Cup.

The team bus driving into Kaiserslautern for the match against Japan to discover a city of green and gold, World Cup stadiums full of Australian supporters, and… the noise.

"Hearing the national anthem sung before the Japan game, with 20,000 Australians singing, was phenomenal," Arnold recalled. "And the last 10 minutes of the Japan game was a massive emotional roller coaster. Down 1-0 and knowing that we had to win to stand a chance of going through to the last 16."

Then there was the performance against Brazil and the dramatic night in Stuttgart against Croatia.

"No one expected us to get through but the way the boys performed that night was magnificent. I don't like to single out players but Harry Kewell that night…"

Arnold paused.

"After the Croatia game, no one left the stadium and to celebrate with all the supporters was fantastic. You can't even look back with any bitterness or sadness about the Italy game although it was an unfortunate way to finish. We're a drama queen of a national team. We don't do anything by half-measures. We always leave everything until the last minute and let the whole nation sit on the edge of their seats. We do it that way when we win and we do that when we lose. That could be why I have so many grey hairs."

Yes, 2006 was some year. But that was then. The ball continues to roll. Facing 2007, Arnold now finds himself as national coach - until Frank Lowy finally recruits the international superstar to lead the team that he so keenly seeks. Arnold, however, is not fazed by the reality of being Lowy's make-do second choice, instead relishing the opportunity to take the Socceroos into Asia next year.

"I am coach of the Socceroos and we are doing it my way for an interim period," Arnold said. "How long will it go on for? I can't tell you but I'm doing the best possible job I can do. I've had a very good discussion with Frank Lowy and John O'Neill, before he left, and [FFA Head of High Performance] John Boultbee and I know my situation can change any day. But it's not about me. It's about the national teams. I could have taken the easy option and walked away when Guus Hiddink went and, on the back of being an assistant who got to the last 16 of the World Cup, moved on somewhere else. But I can see what the future is and the transition period that we are in."

Arnold may be taking a role as Lowy's football mistress but that doesn't mean he hasn't been allowed to decorate the house. A good performance at the Asian Cup next year is a priority, alongside renovations to the squad.

"The Australian public now expects," Arnold said. "One thing I have pushed hard is that, previously, if Harry Kewell and Mark Viduka didn't turn up, we were called a second-rate national team. But we've now gone to another level where all the players are household names. I'm going to the Asian Cup to make the semifinals - minimum. For the 2010 World Cup, we have to be in the top four in Asia. If we can use the Asian Cup as a trial and get to the semi-finals, then we will be in a good position for the World Cup campaign."

Arnold's role has changed more than just in job title. As an assistant for seven years, the former Socceroo striker was doorman for Frank Farina and Guus Hiddink, the players' go-to man and immune from tough decisions. Now, Arnold can make or break careers.

"I'd been the good cop for six years but I had to be the bad cop straight away," Arnold said. "The players tested me when I took over but that's what players are like. But it wasn't hard because I have ambition to coach and go overseas again one day. I was one of the first to play overseas and I would like to do the same as a coach."

Arnold expects the recent international retirement of Tony Vidmar, Stan Lazaridis, Zeljko Kalac and Tony Popovic to be mirrored after the Asian Cup by potentially five more players.

But impressed by leadership roles played by Lucas Neill, Vince Grella, and Tim Cahill since the World Cup he suggests the current overhaul is part of developing a successful squad.

"The worst thing would have been if nine or 10 of the team from the World Cup had walked away at the same time," Arnold said. "I managed to convince half a dozen to stay on. Then they can make another decision after the Asian Cup. I have given the older guys jobs as mentors, to talk to the younger ones at dinner and at lunch and make them feel comfortable in the squad and even coach them on the pitch. If there are another four or five retirements after the Asian Cup then we're in good shape. The older group – Bresciano, Grella, Emerton, Kewell, Cahill, Culina – will be around 30 in 2010. But we need guys like Brett Holman, Patrick Kisnorbo, Nathan Burns and David Williams to come through and step up."

A GALAXY WITH ONE STAR AND THE TEAMMATES JUST WANT DINNER

Los Angeles, January 2007

One week after the announcement David Beckham will join Los Angeles Galaxy later this year and the Californian club's office is still buzzing.

"He's not even arrived yet and it has gone crazy," said Galaxy coach Frank Yallop.

Sitting in small office under the Home Depot Center's main stand (Galaxy's stadium is sponsored by a home renovation store) Yallop had the honour of adding Beckham's name to his whiteboard during the week.

"It is still disbelief and an eye-opening experience for everyone here," Yallop said. "When you sign any sort of player it's always good but someone like David Beckham? He is a real eye spinner. He's a global superstar. I haven't met him yet but I have spoken to him briefly and he seems a really nice fella. I hear nothing but good things"

No doubt, Beckham would have been pleased to talk to Yallop on the phone. The five-year deal that brought the former England captain to the United States has been reported as worth US$250 million. A fair swag of that figure is incentive-based and related to endorsements but the size of the deal is huge, even in comparison with heavyweight US sports like American football, basketball, and baseball.

"For the first time there are people attaching Major League Soccer to the mainstream sports landscape," said Allen Hopkins, a soccer analyst for ESPN. "Beckham has provided instant notoriety, credibility, and star power. He transcends the sport and this has become a front-page story. Not just of newspapers but entertainment outlets like Variety."

Hopkins knows the value of star power in the United States. As a producer of Hollywood soccer blockbuster movie Goal! - in which Beckham starred as himself - Hopkins sees a direct link between sport and the entertainment industry.

Beckham's impending arrival even earned a skit on institutional TV show Saturday Night Live: "In soccer news, a team called Los Angeles Galaxy actually exists," joked comedian Amy Poehler on the program last weekend.

"We now have all these eyes on the sport and the question is, now what do we do?" Hopkins said. "Can we capitalise on the momentum that Beckham is going to bring and create a product that is sustainable?"

Hopkins, however, issues a yellow card to other developing leagues - such as Australia's A-League – that may consider rushing to follow MLS footsteps and sign golden tent marquee players like Beckham.

"Beckham would not have happened in the MLS a few years ago," he said. "Soccer did not have the infrastructure in place that we take for granted in the other sports like baseball, NFL, and NBA. The MLS had to start from scratch ten years ago."

Hopkins also suggests the boom-bust era of 1970s NASL that saw New York Cosmos sign Pele and Franz Beckenbauer and then disappear into a well of debt will not repeat.

"This time we have real clubs with real money," he said. "The ownership group in MLS is a who's who of sports business in this country. It's not someone's pet project. The people are legitimate and not going to let that happen again."

While Galaxy's office hummed with congratulatory calls and requests for interviews from around the world, on the fields outside the stadium, the US national team was preparing for this weekend's friendly with Denmark.

Post-World Cup, the USA is in a similar situation as Australia. Bob Bradley, a former MLS coach, has been appointed to take the team until a permanent successor to Bruce Arena can be found. Negotiations with Germany's World Cup coach Jurgen Klinsmann broke down last December and, with this weekend's game not scheduled on an official FIFA date, Bradley leads an under-strength squad of local players for his international debut. The Beckham buzz had not passed by Bradley, however.

"There are so many sports here in the US and so many superstar athletes that sometimes the battle to move soccer up the ladder in the public eye is difficult," said Bradley.

"If Beckham can help accelerate this process and show people around the world that the game here is important and improving every day that would be great."

Beckham's wife, former pop star Victoria, spent the past week in Los Angeles eating at restaurants with Tom Cruise and Katie Holmes and house hunting for a Stateside Beckingham Palace.

Should Victoria choose to establish home base in Beverly Hills or fashionable upscale Brentwood, her husband's daily commute for training at the Galaxy's headquarters in Carson will give the superstar a true LA experience. Galaxy's current biggest name, Landon Donovan lives nearby Home Depot Centre at Manhattan Beach but Beckham's possible sweep down the 101 or 405 freeway will take him from the glamorous end of town through fabled lower end areas like South Central LA and Compton.

On good day, Beckham can expect to travel one hour each way but freeway congestion will extend his journey to a possible four hour round trip. Amid the big money talk, such trivialities can be overlooked but Frank Yallop is confident he will keep his small 18-man squad focused despite the extra attention the team will receive.

"I have to make sure that he integrates with the team," Yallop said. "All I really care about is winning games on the field. All the other stuff is irrelevant to me as long as my players don't get into trouble and are not getting picked on outside of the game."

Last season, Galaxy's entire salary budget was US$2.1 million, split between 25 players. Beckham will earn the equivalent of that in two weeks.

"He has always been one of the highest earners at every club he has been with because he is marketable," Yallop said. "I don't think any of the players will have any jealousy at all because if they could earn what he does they would. The whole package with Beckham is so big that we won't fully realise the extent of it until he actually arrives. It's good for us because it has given us a good lift. We feel proud that he has chosen to come to the US and play for the Galaxy."

But like many players, Galaxy defender and US international Chris Albright was pragmatic about Beckham's arrival.

"I just hope he buys dinner a few times," he said.

SOME OF THEM...
THEY ARE GOING TO BE KILLED

Amman, June 2007

If Socceroo coach Graham Arnold feels he has big challenges ahead of the upcoming Asian Cup, he may consider a thought for his Iraqi counterpart, Jorvan Vieira. Vieira, a 53-year-old Brazilian, was appointed Iraq's coach just two weeks ago. His family remains at home in Morocco while his team assembles at a makeshift base in Amman, Jordan.

Vieira has a colourful resumé. He was an assistant coach with Morocco at the 1986 World Cup – the first African team to make the second round – and has extensive experience with Arabic clubs and national teams. Yet nothing has quite prepared him for steering Iraq at its first Asian Cup appearance in 20 years.

"You cannot imagine it," Vieira said after dinner at an Amman restaurant on Thursday with his players, officials from the Iraq federation, and a team sponsor – an international electrical goods company sees leverage in Iraq despite the troubles.

"I am in a real Arabic souk," he explained. "Every day, I don't know where we will go for training. Every day, people want to meet with me for two or three hours a day to discuss the players. Today, I kicked a chair. I kicked everything!"

Frustrated, Vieira explained the reality for a team with no home, representing a broken country.

"There is no organisation," he said. "Nothing. I have to understand why, however, because the kind of life these people are living, they don't have a home. The people who represent the federation are living in Amman. Some of them, if they go to Iraq, they are going to be killed."

"When you don't know where your home is, where your things are, you are lost in space. It's the same when you have no organisation in your house. You don't know where you put your socks or your trousers. It's the same here. They are lost people because of the war. This is the reality."

Carrying an Iraqi passport, even if you're a player for the national team, can lead to situations other professional footballers, with their first-class flights and culture of bling, may struggle to comprehend.

"Some players arrived here in Amman a few days ago and they had to wait six or seven hours at the airport," Vieira explained. "The Jordanian police would not allow them to come into the country. Nobody did anything, nobody moved, nobody wrote a list of players to tell the government that this is the Iraq national team. The players suffered only because they had Iraq passports. But they are just people."

Vieira's scattered squad has arrived in Amman from Iraq, Lebanon, Cyprus, and Iran. He said that, as individuals, the team was no different to other players he had coached: Brazilians, Moroccans, and Malaysians. No different, that is, except these players have had their homeland shattered.

"I don't have one person in this group who hasn't lost someone from their family because of this war," Vieira said. "But they never mix politics in the team. They never talk about it. They regret the situation, of course, and they are nostalgic. They miss their country and they're not happy to see their country like it is but nobody talks about the war."

"I have different boys here, different groups, different sects, like in Iraq, but here nothing happens and everything is OK. I have Sunni and I have Shi'a and there is no problem. They are very close."

"I have experience with a lot of Arabic countries and I have learned a lot since I've been with the Iraq team. This is a typical religious war. The extremists have tried to put more fire in the situation. Iraqi people who used to live in peace before, and had respect for religious differences, are now under oppression."

Vieira also has the small matter of a tournament for which he was hired to ensure Iraqi success. His team will meet Thailand in its opening game before closing the group stage against Oman, a country Vieira has previously coached. In between is tournament favourite Australia.

"I'm planning to go as far as possible," Vieira said. "I'm not looking for first place in our group but I want second place. Australia has a lot of chances to come top."

Ah, the Socceroos.

"I didn't say that I am going to lose against Australia," Vieira said, with a smile. "I didn't say that."

He then unveiled a detailed list of facts, figures, and statistics about Australia and its players, including the ins and outs and positives and negatives of Mark Viduka's transfer to Newcastle United and a detailed analysis of the striker's hesitation in committing to the Asian Cup.

"I have everything in my files," Vieira said.

He even spent the previous night watching Australia's Olympic team beat Jordan in a Beijing qualifying match in Amman. Mark Milligan, that team's captain and also named in Arnold's squad, now features in Vieira's dossier.

Iraq's coach nods.

"I took some notes."

Postscript: Two weeks after this interview, Iraq beat Australia 3-1 in its Asian Cup group game. Vieira led Iraq to the final, where his team beat Saudi Arabia 1-0.

FABIO CAPELLO IS "ADDED TO THE PROCESS"

Rome, November 2007

In November 2007, Dick Advocaat guided Zenit St Petersburg to their first league title since 1984 with a win over Saturn Moscow. The Dutchman was thrown in the air by celebrating players and came back to earth with a bump and an offer for a one-year contract extension worth $4 million after tax. Considering the offer, Advocaat did what many men in his position might have. He switched off his mobile phone.

Meanwhile, on the other side of the world, several Australians were trying to call Advocaat. To offer congratulations on his win, but also to firm up their plans for the next seven days. The idea was that the man who had previously coached PSV, Rangers, Borussia Monchengladbach, the Netherlands, South Korea, and the United Arab Emirates, would be officially unveiled as Australia's new coach before their friendly with Nigeria in London. Three months after Advocaat signed a contract to lead the Socceroos to the 2010 World Cup, Football Federation Australia were eager to make public the worst-kept secret in Australian football.

But Advocaat's phone stayed off. And off. And still off. The only person willing to talk about an increasingly uncomfortable situation was Zenit's technical director, Konstantin Sarsania, who was sure that Advocaat would not be heading for Bondi Beach any time soon. The $4 million a year on offer from a club sponsored by state gas utility Gazprom - double what the Australians would and could pay - would solve that.

As late as Friday lunchtime before the Saturday game against Nigeria in London, Australian officials were claiming Advocaat was still due to arrive. Later that afternoon, however, the conversation between players at the team hotel was that Advocaat had officially been renamed "Dastardly Dick". The players had it right. Australia were left coachless heading toward the start of World Cup qualifiers.

Advocaat's snub came on the back of an embarrassingly lame Australian performance at the 2007 Asian Cup, where a team led by Graham Arnold bowed out in the quarter-finals after losing to Iraq and failing to beat Oman. The 2006 World Cup exploits had left an enormous hangover.

"The World Cup had a huge impact on the players, the supporters, and the nation," captain Lucas Neill explained. "It really made soccer popular in Australia. However, after the Guus Hiddink era, we've plateaued and possibly even gone back a tiny bit... We want stability, continuity, and cohesion. As a player, you want to be settled. You want to know what is right and wrong. In all football, whether you agree or disagree with it, so long as a coach has a style you know, that if you're doing what he tells you to do, then you are doing the right thing."

After the World Cup, Australia lost Hiddink to the riches of the Russian national team, so Arnold, an assistant to both Hiddink and the Dutchman's predecessor Frank Farina, took charge of the Socceroos – sort of.

The Asian Cup came with divisions within the camp – unusual in a squad that had previously prided itself on unified camaraderie. Post-tournament, many players privately said Arnold, who had spells as a player in Holland and Belgium, was not up to the task of managing a team with experienced players at European clubs.

FFA officials, meanwhile, spent the week after Advocaat's snub criss-crossing Europe speaking with potential new candidates. The wish list (official and unofficial) ran from José Mourinho (he was unemployed) to Jürgen Klinsmann (FFA technical director Rob Baan named the German as a contender).

Klinsmann's interest had roots in a 2007 meeting in Los Angeles with Peter Lowy, son of Frank and co-CEO of the Westfield Corporation. Klinsmann was then hot off taking Germany to the semi-finals of the 2006 World Cup and interested in a new project. FFA thought Klinsmann had some good credentials. Peter Lowy did dad's bidding over lunch at a trendy LA restaurant.

"Real estate was one subject they discussed but coaching opportunities with Australia were tossed around," said one person privy to the conversation at the time. A sticking point was Klinsmann's insistence on living in California - as he'd done while coaching Germany. Australia wanted its coach to live in the beachside apartment in Sydney's Manly that it could provide. Klinsmann stayed in California to take over the USA national team.

Fabio Capello and Jorvan Vieira (he'd won the Asian Cup with Iraq) were other interested names while at the same time one local flag-waving journalist to reinstate Arnold (most felt no Australian is up to the task).

As FFA tried to negotiate a compensation package from Zenit, Australia took some solace in knowing they weren't alone being jilted by Advocaat. In 2005, he'd quit his job with the United Arab Emirates to take over South Korea, leaving his car keys with his hotel reception and catching a cab to the airport for a flight to Seoul. His UAE bosses didn't know he'd left them until they read about it in a newspaper.

Fabio Capello's interest in the Australia job was long standing. When Australia was eliminated from the Asian Cup, an email arrived in my inbox: "Would Australia be interested in Capello?"

A long-time friend of Capello explained the Italian was looking for a new challenge. Maybe Europe. Maybe the USA. Maybe a club. Maybe a national team. Australia held definite interest.

A message was sent to the FFA. Confidentiality assured, would they like to pursue the opportunity?

Australia didn't rush to reply but another message from Italy was forwarded to Sydney. On Capello's return from his summer vacation, he would even be happy to travel to Australia to meet. No response from Australia but, meanwhile, the Italian travelled to London for a meeting with the president of the US Soccer Federation. Capello was clearly seriously considering options. It wasn't until early September that a text message confirmed FFA had passed on meeting Capello: "Timing delays have blown it out."

Fast-forward two months, the day before Australia was to play Nigeria in London. FFA finally conceded Advocaat was staying in Russia. That same afternoon, another email. Capello was still interested in Australia. FFA was again informed. Australian bosses said they were meeting on Monday to draw up a new short list and, if Capello was of interest, they said they knew where to find me.

Monday, nothing. Tuesday, nothing. Wednesday, Croatia beat England, Steve McClaren was sacked, and European football went nuts. As FFA trawled Europe for its own headline-grabbing high-profile coach, big name candidates, including Jurgen Klinsmann and a reengaged Guus Hiddink, now had a new option - England.

So, too, had Capello, but the Italian maintained interest in the Socceroos. Another message from Italy: he was available to meet in Europe immediately. Australia stayed silent. Yet another message from the Italians: is Australia interested or not? Finally, John Boultbee, then FFA's head of high performance, offered a reply: Capello had been added to "the process".

I had spent the week after Australia's game against Nigeria in Rome. The Friday night November air was cool but that didn't keep locals or tourists away from the outside restaurant tables that line the Campo de Fiori. The week was winding down but my phone buzzing in my jacket pocket suggested my glass of red wine was going to be more business than pleasure. The call was from FFA CEO Ben Buckley. Apparently, I now had something he wanted - an as-good-as-it-gets solution to the Socceroos' coaching conundrum.

"I believe you can put us in touch with Fabio Capello," Buckley said.

He was right. after all, I had been waiting - along with the former Juventus, Milan and Réal Madrid coach - for a call since July. Now, Buckley wanted to talk. Urgently. He was flying from London to Sydney the following morning but would welcome the chance to talk with Capello.

"There are no agents involved here," I explained. "This is a direct line to his family." Buckley joked after he had been jilted by Advocaat: "So long as he can sign a contract and stick to it."

Dots were joined and on the Saturday morning, after Buckley watched the Italian interviewed on BBC TV about his interest in the now vacant England job, a call finally took place with Capello's lawyer son. On Tuesday someone within FFA broke confidentiality and leaked Capello's interest in Australia to a newspaper. The story was true but already out of date. Capello was genuine but there were now other opportunities offering more than the $2.17 million a year – plus a Sydney apartment – that Australia touted.

Money aside, Capello's other important issue: World Cup qualification is a tough task. Australia had great players but the Socceroos were not playing Fiji any more. Whoever took the job had to be an expert in Asia. I called Jorvan Vieira in Casablanca, Morocco. Vieira was the man who coached Iraq to victory at the Asian Cup. He was sitting in the green room of a TV station when I rang him. We spoke about his recent successful Asian Cup campaign leading Iraq to a historic triumph, along the way beating Graham Arnold's Australia 3-1.

"I'm not going to judge another coaching colleague or professional players," Vieira said about the Socceroos. "Unless you're inside the family you don't know the problems."

Vieira was born near Rio de Janeiro to a Portuguese father and Brazilian mother and is married to a Moroccan. He spoke seven languages, held a PhD in sports science and knew how to win in Asia. When I asked him how Australia could win the first phase of its 2010 World Cup qualifying group that featured China, Iraq, and Qatar, he said: "The first match against China will decide the qualification. This is a short tournament, not a league. If you drop points early it's difficult to recover."

"Whatever coach Australia takes has to have experience in Asia. Don't think about the big names," he said. "I hear about Klinsmann and Capello. They are fantastic for the marketing department but we're not looking for marketing. We're looking for results."

Vieira never spoke to anyone from FFA. He was - of course - interested in the Australian job but, like Capello, if his phone never rang, he had no shortage of opportunities elsewhere: national teams, clubs, TV stations.

As we learned in a very short time, outside Australia, the world game can turn unexpectedly - and quickly.

MARK SHIELD IS A REFEREE – AND A HUMAN BEING

Brisbane, November 2007

Let's go straight to the question every Australian fan might like to ask the country's best football referee. Would Mark Shield, wearer of a FIFA badge and who oversaw several matches in Germany in June, have awarded Italy that penalty? Professionalism versus patriotism? Come on, Mr Shield. Give it up. He has an answer. Sort of.

"If I was the referee, I think I would have made the same decision as [Luis Medina Cantalejo] did at the time," said Shield. But as thousands of Socceroos fans gasp in shock, Shield revealed that referees might just be human after all.

"Then, I would have looked at the replay and gone 'Possibly not'. The Lucas Neill tackle was one of those ones that could have gone either way. There is no doubt about that."

"If you look at the incident, the referee whistled straight away and he believed in his mind that it was a penalty. But if you look on replay, from a number of different angles, it is possible it wasn't. It was a very difficult decision in a live situation."

A tough call, but as Shield admits, that's why the men in the middle are the whistleblowers and we, mere mortals, shout at both them and television sets.

As Australia's top match official, the 33-year-old has credentials and experience. The Queenslander made his World Cup Finals debut in 2002 in Japan and most recently took charge of the second-leg of the Asian Champions League Final earlier this month between Syrian side Al Karama and South Korea's Jeonbuk Motors.

That match was, literally, a long way from the A-League games he referees each week. A flight to Damascus and three-hour car trip gave some indication of what Sydney and Adelaide United will experience next year on their own Asian adventure. A stadium of

40,000 local fans watched Al Karama pull back a two-goal deficit from the first leg before the Koreans scored a last-minute winner to dramatically snatch the trophy.

"The people in Syria were just great: lovely, friendly, football loving people and the atmosphere at the game itself was fantastic," Shield said. "When they came back to 2-2 and I blew my whistle I couldn't hear it. That is how loud it was. Then when the Koreans scored it went so quiet, I could hear my pen click when I wrote down the scorer."

Refereeing found Shield (rather than Shield finding refereeing) when he was playing - occasionally - for his local under-12 team in Brisbane. He often struggled to get a game in the junior side and when a referee needed two volunteer assistants, teammates had no hesitation in pointing at left-out Shield.

"I was destined to be a referee," Shield said. "A referee came across and asked for two linesman and all the players looked at me: you do it - you're not going to get a game. I fell in love with it instantly. I mean, who gets excited about running up and down the sideline? I did the course a weekend after and then refereed an under-7 match."

Just ten years later, Shield took charge of his first top-level match, a National Soccer League encounter between Sydney United - featuring Sydney's David Zdrilic and Mark Rudan in its line-up - and West Adelaide.

"I was very nervous," Shield said. "It was on TV. When the captains came up I pushed my chest out and tried to look like I was in control and calm and not nervous at all. Sydney United's captain Velimir Kupresak came up at the coin toss and said, 'Does your mum know you are out?' I went to pieces but I got over the nerves and it went OK."

Two World Cups later, Shield said man management skills and, unsurprisingly, the ability to get decisions right are key to good refereeing.

"If out of 100 decisions you get 99 of them wrong it doesn't matter how good your man management skills are," Shield said. "You must be able to handle the players, too. Show empathy and show that you are in control. If players have confidence in you then it becomes easy."

Although fans, and some players, might be incredulous, the past World Cup saw referees put through a rigorous fitness and training program. For A-League matches, Shield will train four days a week but the World Cup saw officials workout daily.

"We would train three or four hours a day, 90 minutes physical and 90 minutes practical," Shield said. "Do we practice holding up yellow cards and blowing a whistle? Yes. Everyday."

"The World Cup is a lot of pressure. There are 64 matches and a lot of people watching. It was very successful for the referees. There were matches that didn't go that well and there were some decisions that were either wrong or certainly contentious but there were less mistakes than in 2002."

Even with high stakes, Shield is reluctant to see video technology employed in matches.

"Video might have some use but it's very difficult because football is such a free flowing game," Shield said.

He would, however, see benefit in video helping to stamp out the scourge of the sport - diving.

"One thing that FIFA have to look at is simulation," Shield said. "Players falling to the ground with little or no contact. It's very hard for the referee to see it because it happens so quickly. I don't think a referee can be blamed when players are diving all over the place and makes a mistake with a foul when it wasn't."

Shield would like to see harder penalties for simulation - current laws suggest a caution in addition to a free kick for 'unsporting behaviour'.

"It is a real blight on the game," he said.

"What frustrates referees is when we do a video review of the game and we got it wrong and the player has clearly dived to the ground and got a penalty or we have a sent a guy off. Live, at the time, it clearly looked like a penalty."

HARRY KEWELL WILL ARRIVE IN PRECISELY 13 MINUTES

Manchester, July 2008

Harry Kewell spent this weekend holidaying in California and contemplating contract offers from clubs in England, Italy, Turkey, Greece and Russia. Yet, as Kewell readily admits, his future would offer fewer exotic options if not for the work of Australian physiotherapist Les Gelis, who nursed the former Liverpool player back to fitness after four years of injury hell.

"Without a doubt, if it wasn't for Les, I wouldn't be here," Kewell says. "He's the one person who's made sure that I'm back. There's probably only one person who knows me better inside and out, and that's my wife."

Let's get the awkward part out of the way early. Harry Kewell spent five years at Liverpool, a spell that tossed up medals for winning the UEFA Champions League and FA Cup. This was also five years that will forever be known as a time when debilitating injuries stopped Australia's most talented footballer from perhaps being the truly great player, he seemed destined to be.

Five seasons, 138 first team games and 16 goals were outweighed by several operations, countless hours in the gym, and a handful of not-quite-there comebacks.

It wasn't until Gelis took control of Kewell's rehabilitation at Liverpool that progress was made. The upshot? Liverpool subsequently hired the Socceroo physio to take care of the club's other injured players which says much about the club's ability to fix a prized possession at the time. Nevertheless, we would all agree, even with Liverpool medals and a Socceroos highlight reel featuring that goal against Croatia in Stuttgart, that the past few years didn't go quite according to plan. But what did Kewell learn from his time at Anfield?

"I know all the muscles in my groin, I can tell you that," Kewell says. "And I can tell you how to take criticism."

He pauses.

"You know what?" His mind ticks over. "Liverpool is a great club and they have a great fan base. Let's just leave it at that."

Gelis has worked with the Socceroos since 1997 when Kewell burst on the international scene but the 38-year-old plays down his role in saving the career of Australia's most talented player.

"Harry is the most consummate professional," Gelis says. "If he says he'll meet you in 13 minutes, he's there in 13 minutes. He's one of those guys who if he had to pay his way around the world to compete for free, he'd do that. It's almost a privilege to work with someone so committed."

Gelis sees the Socceroos captain playing for years to come after injuries truly threatened to prematurely end the 29-year-old's career. Several operations corrected problems that doctors originally misdiagnosed. Gelis would often spend seven hours a day with Kewell working on rehabilitation.

"A significant part of rehab is mental," Gelis says. "Take the top two percent of all international footballers and, to a man, you'll find it's their mental prowess that keeps them at the top level. There are a lot of players who are immensely talented who fall by the wayside."

One of Gelis' greatest challenges was getting Kewell fit for the 2006 World Cup after Australia's star was injured playing for Liverpool in the FA Cup final that year. Alongside fitness coach Anthony Crea, Gelis worked overtime to deliver Kewell to Guus Hiddink for Australia's first game of the tournament against Japan. Talk to coaching staff now and they admit that Kewell played the tournament "on one leg".

"Hiddink used to say, 'This is the World Cup, take a risk'," Gelis says of the pressure to get players on the pitch. Reward came with Kewell's dramatic goal against Croatia to send Australia into the knockout stages but the physio says satisfaction comes from smaller things.

"I'd like to think Harry scored that goal against Croatia because he's the player, not because of anything that I necessarily did. There's more satisfaction in my role seeing a player run around in a game. It's also little things like when a player is able to complete a training session or gets selected in a team."

The work of Gelis and Crea at the 2006 World Cup was the culmination of a somewhat radical program that began two years earlier. Football Federation Australia based the fitness gurus in Britain to be closer to European-based Australian players and to improve diplomacy with clubs. The concept, first raised by Socceroos coach Terry Venables in 1997 and later championed by Frank Farina, was only introduced when Frank Lowy's new administration found the funds.

"It was all about diplomacy," Gelis says. "It was a softly, softly, approach initially. I can only think of one situation where there was a little bit of friction with a club but the rest went extremely well."

After working with Liverpool, Gelis ran a private practice in Manchester catering for elite athletes.

"There's a lot that is unknown to the public about what happened with Harry," he says. "A lot of assertions got made and there was a lot of misinformation. There's been a lot of adversity. I have a lot of sympathy for what he's been through. His determination was a big factor in coming back."

A DINNER WITH FRANK LOWY AND JACK WARNER

Somewhere in the Caribbean Sea, December 2008

As 2008 eased into 2009, Frank Lowy's luxury yacht nudged a course through the Caribbean Sea toward Trinidad & Tobago. Lowy is the 78-year-old chairman of Football Federation Australia and one of the richest people in the country, mainly due to his vast Westfield shopping-centre empire that reaches across the United States, Great Britain, Australia, and New Zealand. But while Lowy no doubt enjoyed the Caribbean New Year sun, he had another reason for visiting the West Indies. After all, during a Sydney summer, most people would not begrudge him staying home at his Sydney harbourside mansion.

Lowy was keen to keep his travel plans quiet but Jack Warner, the controversial FIFA vice-president from Trinidad & Tobago who will have influence in where the 2018 World Cup will be held, was not so shy.

"I know Frank Lowy very well and I am planning to have dinner with him as his yacht visits the Caribbean," Warner explained.

Let the lobbying begin for the 2018 World Cup begin. In December, Australia officially entered the race to host 2018 World Cup when the government pledged AUS$45.6 million to fund a lobbying campaign for two years. Australia's pitch to win 13 of FIFA's 24 executive committee votes hangs on what it considers to be, according to one insider, a "formidable management team" of Lowy and his chief executive officer, Ben Buckley, a former Australian rules footballer and an experienced sports administrator.

Part of Football Federation Australia's campaign will include the message that Australia, a member of the Asian Football Confederation, is geographically in the world's fastest-growing football market and economy (pay attention: that's Asia). FFA has done its numbers and, quietly, already counts nine votes in its corner – one from Oceania, four from Asia, and four from Africa, even though that region receives considerable funding from UEFA.

What is needed for 2018 to head down under, suggest sources, is a split from either UEFA, South America (likely to vote for Spain-Portugal), or Warner's Concacaf. And here's where it gets complicated and interesting.

"Let me tell you this – Australia is now a member of the Asian Football Confederation and Asia just hosted the World Cup in 2002 in Japan and Korea," Warner said before he met Lowy. "Normally, the World Cup must go to different Confederations, so why would it go back to Asia just 16 years after it has been held there? If Australia had stayed in Oceania then we could say that Oceania has never had the World Cup and then there could be no question that Australia deserves to host in 2018."

As well as Australia, Warner's views would not have been well received in Japan, which is considering a 2018 bid, nor in Qatar, which is also keen to join the fray despite June and July not being the most pleasant months to be in the Middle East (all this as Mohamed Bin Hammam, the AFC's president, said they would support only one Asian bid). But Warner's voting bloc may not be Australia's greatest obstacle. While the Australian government's financial support was celebrated in FFA's Sydney headquarters, not everyone in the country was happy. Some commentators in Australia's mainstream media were in uproar.

"The naive belief that they would ever grant the World Cup to an isolated nation of 20 million people that don't much like soccer in the first place – all in the wrong time zone for prime-time TV in Europe and America – is nothing short of crazy," wrote one of the more measured pundits.

At the Murdoch-run News Limited, which has a large financial stake in Australia's rugby league national competition, the attitude was more aggressive. "While other sports are bleeding and begging the Government for funding, soccer has been handed yet another golden egg," said one columnist. "Staging a World Cup would give soccer bosses the right to trumpet to all of us that this is the only world game and that Australia has a real place in its upper echelons."

Overlooked, or ignored, is that Australia's government considers the AUS$45.6m a good investment when a World Cup bid allows a platform to engage with foreign governments and will also be used as a subtle opportunity to lobby for a place on the United Nations Security Council.

But big pictures are possibly too complicated, or too cumbersome, for a mainstream media that considers hyping the Nicole Kidman film Australia as a national obligation - movie that received $45 million in Australian government grants and was a box-office bomb (except in... Australia). With that all in mind, it's perhaps no wonder that Lowy preferred a Caribbean dinner with Jack Warner over a holiday season at home.

I JUST WANT TO BE THE PERSON THAT I REALLY WAS

Melbourne, January 2009

Ljubo Milicevic was the great white hope of football in Australia. Cut from the same stylish strip as playmakers like Paul Okon and Ned Zelic, Milicevic was a star at Perth Glory, scoring incredible goals in front of 40,000-strong grand final crowds and, and captain of both national youth teams. Ten years ago, Milicevic was destined for the brightest lights in Europe and was touted as a future Socceroos captain. Instead, at what should be the peak of his powers, the 27-year-old is slowly overcoming a battle with depression, playing suburban soccer and working odd jobs.

"Playing for a big club and being at a World Cup was my expectation as well," Milicevic said. "But I can't carry the bitterness around anymore."

It's a long way from appearing in the UEFA Champions League against Thierry Henry to having your A-League contract torn up. But that's exactly what happened to Milicevic. In 2001 he was Australia's captain at the World Youth Cup in Argentina. Poised to sign for German side Hertha Berlin, he blew a knee during the tournament and instead endured 18 months in the wilderness. Instead of Berlin, Milicevic signed for Swiss side FC Zurich, but injured his groin. He then hit form at FC Thun, a modest Swiss club, which led to his appointment as Australia's 2004 Olympic skipper. On Olyroos duty, he again tore his groin. The Olympics in Athens slipped from view.

"I was distraught," Milicevic said. "Injuries stuffed me. Being injured and isolated in a foreign country can bring you down. I also got done over in my first deal in Switzerland and ended up playing on a contract less than what I was getting at Perth Glory. I guess, for many years I was carrying that bitterness."

Oversized success for Thun did little more than mask the signs of depression. The Swiss minnow qualified for the 2005-06 UEFA

Champions League. Milicevic found himself lining up against Henry.

"You can't believe the pressure and what it does to you," he said. "I was walking out at Highbury, playing in the Champions League, and I didn't want to be there."

Depression damaged Milicevic's Socceroos aspirations as well and after he failed to make the final cut for the 2006 World Cup team, he lashed at being left in the wilderness after an impressive season with Thun.

"Being left out is pretty hard to swallow considering the season I've had," Milicevic said at the time. "I had to have a laugh. I'm not that surprised, to be honest. I never had much contact from the national team and I was always pessimistic about the World Cup. My instincts were right. I think people involved have very short memories. I was captain of the under-20s and captain of the Olympic team. I picked up two injuries playing for Australia. I had a horrific run of injuries playing for Australia and came back to fitness to captain my team in Europe but I'm obviously not good enough for Australia. Maybe I should move back to Australia. You seem to have a better chance of playing for Australia if you're playing in the A-League than in the Champions League against Thierry Henry. In Australia, the opponents are obviously better than Thierry Henry. I played Champions League, UEFA Cup and captained my team and that's not good enough? I'm sorry. People I don't know and people who I never expected to hear from say it's bullshit."

In retrospect, Milicevic's raw reaction to being left out of the historic team is simple to see but it also masked a deeper - and often unspoken - issue.

"Guus Hiddink was fantastic," Milicevic explained. "I don't think I've ever worked with a better coach. My problem was that I was going through depression at the time and, again, I didn't want to be there. Hiddink never saw the real me."

When the news broke, he had missed the cut for the 2006 World Cup finals in Germany, Milicevic fled to France. A weekend partying at the Cannes Film Festival flipped into a six-week odyssey that ended up in breakdown.

"I hit the wall again, thinking, 'Where am I? What am I doing here? Where's my family? I'm single. I don't have any kids.' I broke down, I guess. I put weight on. I'm not one of those people who turns to alcohol or drugs. I turn to chocolate and doughnuts. I had days when I would not eat a proper meal. I would go from patisseries, one to the other, eating. I was obviously burnt out. I was going through depression. There is no way around that. But I didn't go and see anyone. Maybe I was too proud. If I'm really honest, it was ongoing since I went overseas."

Brendan Schwab, chief executive of the Australian Professional Footballers Association, believes professional players face unique pressures. "There's a perception that professional footballers are lucky. There's no doubt it's a fantastic career; however, it's extremely tough," he said. "They have to work so hard, physically and mentally. They are among the toughest people. They are extraordinary individuals. Unfortunately, if you're a professional footballer there is only one measure of your self-esteem, and that is the quality of your career, but that's not a real measure of the quality of the person."

Convinced by his family to return to Australia, Milicevic signed for hometown team Melbourne Victory, the A-League champion. Luring home players of his calibre was exactly the A-League blueprint.

"For the first time in my life, I was going to play in front of my family and friends and do everything I could to help Melbourne win another title," Milicevic said.

Things didn't go well. A personality clash with captain Kevin Muscat spread to disenchantment with coaching staff and the club's administration. The final blow was a knee injury in the opening minutes of the season. Milicevic cannot discuss details, honouring an agreement with the club after his contract was terminated, but the unhappy homecoming opened another trapdoor.

"I ate heaps of chocolate, sat on the couch, and watched heaps of DVDs," he said. "I slept at all hours of the day and all hours of the night. I was playing the pokies and wearing tracky-daks and T-shirts with chocolate stains on them. It was all I could do to get by."

Eight months of darkness were lifted by school friend Ricky Diaco, a former Victory player.

"I started working at his garden nursery on the weekends, collecting trolleys and lifting pots for grandmas," Milicevic said. "I'm now training with my junior club, Dandenong City. It's great to be with childhood friends and laugh at training together. I can't remember the last time that happened. I just want to be the person that I really was."

CLUELESS AND THE INTERNATIONAL MAN OF MYSTERY

New York, October 2010

Apparently, I had ruined everything. In isolation, this was not unusual but in this context it was something quite extraordinary. It was a situation that would reveal the weakness of those with fake authority and power and become a masterclass in how not to win friends or influence people. The story begins earlier but we will join it in October 2009 when the *Sydney Morning Herald* and *The Age* published my story that revealed Peter Hargitay - an infamous consultant that had worked for corrupt FIFA officials Sepp Blatter and Mohammed Bin Hammam - was working for Football Federation Australia on its World Cup bid.

The great irony was that this may have been a non-story had Australia's bid admitted Hargitay was on its payroll. When the story was eventually published, FFA CEO Ben Buckley and Australia bid executive Bonita Mersiades were sitting in an airline lounge at Abu Dhabi airport waiting for a connecting flight to Sydney after a trip to Cairo to lobby voters on FIFA's executive committee. After reading the story online, Mersiades called Hargitay who, according to her account in the book *Whatever It Takes – the Inside Story of the 'FIFA Way'*, exploded in a rage to charge that, apparently according to Hargitay, I had indeed ruined everything.

The story was damning of FFA's decision to keep Hargitay's employment a secret. I'd been told 12 months earlier that FFA had hired the Swiss-Hungarian by several independent sources but FFA would not admit to Hargitay having any role with Australia's bid. It was later revealed by Mersiades in her book that this was on the orders of FFA Chairman Frank Lowy and against the advice of Buckley and Mersiades, on more than one occasion. Eventually, I tracked down Hargitay and convinced him to admit he was working for Australia and asked him to answer some questions by email.

Headlined "FFA's International Man of Mystery", the article laid out Hargitay's history and his supposed job with FFA. Some of the background information was well-documented by Andrew Jennings - Hargitay's nemesis - but it was all new to Australian readers that included the federal government and the taxpayers funding the bid and ultimately paying Hargitay his significant fee.

According to FFA, Hargitay's role was to provide "high-level strategy and networking advice and counsel" while Hargitay also claimed to offer FFA "relationship building and advice to the FFA in matters of relevance to Australia's bid for the 2018 and 2022 World Cups".

FFA refuses to reveal how much it is paying Hargitay and his company, European Consultancy Network, even though funding for Australia's World Cup bids comes from a $45.6 million Federal Government grant," the story revealed.

At times elusive and initially reluctant to speak about his role for Australia, Hargitay consented to a rare interview, via email and under strict conditions that his answers be "published in their original form, not shortened, edited or amended in any way, shape or form. If changes are made in one answer, the entire interview MUST NOT be used."

That request was not how editors from Fairfax Media, which published the *Sydney Morning Herald* and *The Age*, or its lawyers operated. It was not how any serious media organisation operated, either. So the story rolled on.

Born in Hungary in 1951, Hargitay is undoubtedly as well connected as his language skills are broad. He speaks fluent English, Hungarian, German, French and, he said, "reasonably fluent in Spanish and have a fair command of Portuguese, get by in Dutch and read/understand Swedish and Romanian. If you want to count Jamaican patois and Swiss German, you can add those to the list as well."

Hargitay grew up in Switzerland where he played football as a junior. He says he still follows FC Basel but is also a season ticket-holder at Chelsea, a team he has followed for the past 10 years.

But importantly, Hargitay was "special adviser" to FIFA president Sepp Blatter, one of the most powerful men in world sport, until December 2007 when he quit that role to work for England's 2018 World Cup bid. Last May, Hargitay narrowly escaped disaster when an earthquake destroyed a Chinese airport from where a private jet he was travelling in had just taken off.

His fellow passengers? Asian Football Confederation president Mohammed Bin Hammam and controversial FIFA vice-president Jack Warner.

The connections firm up.

Hargitay is an adviser to Bin Hammam, who is a close associate of Lowy. Earlier this year, Hargitay oversaw Bin Hammam's bitter, but ultimately successful, election for a place on FIFA's executive committee.

"I have been [Hammam's] adviser for a number of years and enjoy his friendship," Hargitay said. "There are numerous areas where we have worked together over time, primarily pertaining to developing football in Asia, which is his great passion.

"I continue to be close to the AFC president and was happy to assist him and his team during the election for membership in the FIFA executive committee."

The European Consultancy Network was involved in the early stages of England's 2018 bid before Lord Triesman was appointed chairman of their campaign and called for all outside consultants to reapply for their jobs through a tender process.

The European Consultancy Network declined and the Daily Mail reported Hargitay's team lost a "seven-figure contract" (in British pounds) with the Football Association in the process.

Hargitay denies the England deal was that lucrative.

"The seven-figure contract is a myth," he said. "Our initial work was in the high five figures and would have been in the six over a period of two years.

"We received a fee of £75,000 ($134,000) plus expenses for the first phase of our work; upon conclusion and delivery of the strategic plan, we received a further £25,000 fee. As for Australia, our contract is less than that.

"After we concluded our work for the England bid, we were approached by several countries, none of which we were interested to work for," Hargitay added. "We put a proposal to the FFA, which was accepted and ECN and I were asked to join them as consultants."

The story detailed his history working for Union Carbide, the company whose 1984 factory meltdown in India killed at least 3000 people and with Marc Rich, a US tax-fraud felon, one of America's most wanted, and notorious as a sanctions-buster during South Africa's apartheid regime. It detailed his arrest and acquittal of cocaine trafficking by Jamaican police, and his seven months in prison as a flight risk after being charged and later acquitted with conspiracy to import 18 kilograms of cocaine to the United States.

"It was indeed 'something of an experience,'" Hargitay said when asked if there was anything positive to take from that period in his life.

"Yet, what happened 11 years ago has no bearing on my work and 'acquitted of all charges' is an accurate summary of what happened. Other than that, I see no reason to revisit a matter ad nauseam where I won and powerful people who tried to frame me lost. The facts speak for themselves."

In 1999, Hargitay was employed by Swiss company ABI, which claimed to specialise in "covert operations assignments", according to its website.

A European Consultancy Network website, since shut down, once claimed to help clients "stay out of the media" ... "and to prepare such briefs, news items and alternative scoops that would divert, detract and destabilise imminent media interest."

Outside of football, the European Consultancy Network's clients include a Swiss private bank with interests in the Middle East and, in an amazing turn of events after his earlier legal drama in the country, Hargitay is now an adviser to Jamaica's Minister for Transport and Works, as well as a member of Switzerland's federal parliament, among others. He recently earned PR points for his idea to hand out show bags advertising Australia's bid at a recent football industry convention in London. As for Australia's chances in 2018 or 2022, what feedback has Hargitay received from FIFA's executive committee?

"I understand that Australia's technical bid team have made the best impression of all," he said. "They always meet all the deadlines, they are disciplined, attend all relevant FIFA meetings, deliver all requested materials in a complete manner and have demonstrated a determination and skills that have impressed many at FIFA."

Already well connected to FIFA's executive committee – the 24 men who vote for World Cup hosts – through his place on the organising committee for the 2010 FIFA World Cup, FFA chairman Frank Lowy would not comment on Hargitay's appointment.

In a statement, FFA confirmed the consultancy network had been working for Australia since January, adding, "FFA does not disclose the detail of arrangements with consultants."

"I probably did rather well over time, which is why the trust grew and so did the quality and intensity of my mandate," Hargitay said, when asked of his key relationship with FIFA president Blatter. "Whether my work for FIFA and its president was an important role, as you say, is not something I would want to qualify in those terms."

As well as Hargitay's evasiveness, Chairman Frank Lowy's lack of acknowledgement FFA had him on the books raised red flags about how the organisation was running its bid. I told Mersiades in January 2009 – nine months earlier – that I knew Hargitay was on board. When Mersiades told Ben Buckley, FFA's CEO, he apparently replied: "Shit. How long do you think the fact that Hargitay is working for us will be kept quiet?"

The answer was *too long*. Another can of worms was opened when it became clear I was close to revealing Hargitay's role. It took rumours that I was about to break the story in the *Sydney Morning Herald* and *The Age* for Hargitay and Les Murray, the SBS television celebrity who had editorial control over the TV station's football website The World Game, to break their own version of the news and come clean. Yet they couldn't even do that right.

In an flaccid attempt to spoil my story The World Game published a puff piece written about Hargitay that hit the internet a few hours before Fairfax published my take on Hargitay's role and FFA's silence: "In a major coup, Football Federation Australia have engaged one of football's foremost political strategists to help their bid to bring the World Cup to Australia in either 2018 or 2022. The World Game can exclusively reveal that Peter Hargitay, one-time special adviser to FIFA president Sepp Blatter, and still a close confidant of football's global boss, is now on the FFA payroll as its most important strategy consultant."

The story was so gushing readers may have needed a bucket to mop it up. Many people could be excused for thinking Hargitay had written it himself but - surely - a media outlet like SBS TV must have had enough internal checks and balances to ensure that would never happen. As it was, a broadcast interview that was recorded by Murray was never shown, apparently because even Lowy realised how bad it looked. As it turned out, Murray would be proven to be Hargitay's chief champion and blur the lines between his editorial role at SBS, his relationship with Hargitay, and trumpeting Australia's bid for the World Cup. The saga would not end with much dignity.

Murray agreed with Hargitay's claim that I'd ruined everything. It was made clear to me that anything I wrote about Australia's World Cup bid that that questioned its merits and strategy or strayed from cheerleading would never be published on The World Game - a website I'd written for since it was founded in 2000. It was an extraordinary position for Murray to take, both personally and professionally. He bet his reputation on Hargitay and Frank Lowy and, as the 2022 vote in Zurich and related drama revealed, lost.

Along the way, Murray described journalist Andrew Jennings as a "discredited moron" for his investigations into FIFA. As the FBI and Swiss law enforcement would eventually demonstrate, Jennings was proven to be one of few journalists to be right. After questioning on Twitter the potential for a conflict of interest in being both a supposed journalist and censoring cheerleader, Murray zinged at me: "Don't lecture me on what is a journalist, little boy. I've won awards for it."

Touché!

Having spent time with Murray all over the world, his unconditional support for Hargitay seemed an odd issue to so passionately champion. For someone who had built his career and reputation on celebrating the good and great of football, it seemed most peculiar to now proactively try to shut down anyone querying how Australia's bid was being managed and raising questions about the whole FIFA circus. Something wasn't right - even more so when considering Murray sat on FIFA's Ethics Committee for many years. Mostly, though, the whole episode was just sad.

I wasn't alone. Murray shut down fellow SBS freelancers Jesse Fink and Davidde Corran, both curious and meticulous writers unlikely to transcribe press conferences or press releases. Instead, they scratched into stories that were in the public interest. Fink had credible claims of having his work censored at SBS with direct interference by Murray. Corran, too. After The World Game ran the Hargitay puff piece, Corran wrote about the curiously celebratory profile for another website. Murray sent Corran an email accusing him of discrediting SBS. Murray, obviously, didn't have a mirror.

A few years later the Australian Broadcasting Corporation, a sister station to SBS, looked at Murray's role and the claims he was shutting down alternative views on Australia's bid. SBS denied Murray had a conflict of interest in his role as a journalist while also sitting on a FIFA committee and denied he had censored critique of FIFA or Australia's bid. The catch was there was written evidence to the contrary. I was interviewed by ABC TV researchers for background on their story while Fink and Corran spoke on the record and on camera about their experience. Our freelance contracts were never renewed. We never worked for SBS again.

The episode could be dismissed as media industry gossip except that it revealed how Murray, FFA, and Hargitay had a curious aggressive reaction to anyone who raised questions about Australia's bid or its strategy - or lack of strategy. When it was revealed during the 2010 World Cup in South Africa that the Asian Football Confederation - and by default its Qatari president Mohammed Bin Hammam - had decided to support a European bid for 2018, I wrote that Australia's bid had been caught off guard. We knew this because Frank Lowy and Ben Buckley said so while they were standing in the playground of school in a township outside Johannesburg at an event to promote Australia's bid.

Hargitay was furious at any suggestion he might not be performing at 100 per cent. Having written countless stories that made someone, somewhere, unhappy I had previous experience with people who felt they were wronged - as well as their lawyers. Yet Hargitay was another level. After my analysis of the latest development was published on the politically-centred website Crikey!, widely read in Canberra, Hargitay emailed under the subject heading "Clueless":

"It is your privilege to hyperventilate, invent, fabricate non-stories and offer your clueless bile to readers who deserve better than being exposed to your continued uninformed, unqualified and completely irrelevant blabber. But I have just about had enough of your dim-witted nonsense which is neither based on fact nor has any semblance to logic.

Your total lack of access to any level of decision-making at FIFA (including the janitor), or for that matter to anybody of even minute relevance at FIFA, sheds a deplorable picture on your state of informedness. Not to mention your sorry state of mind.

While cutting a deplorably lonely figure at the USA-Australia friendly, munching away on free sandwiches, you were certainly nowhere near to those who actually understand how this process of bidding works.

I have not once seen you in the lobby of the Michelangelo Hotel nor the Michelangelo Towers in Johannesburg, where all of the decision-makers gather, every day. But then, how would you know? You have no access to the FIFA Club where the FIFA leadership and ExCo Members gather, you cannot access the Michelangelo lobby from the Towers either (you have no accreditation for that move) and you have no idea who is who even if one of the Members were standing in your face.

I have not encountered you once when I spent time with the very same Mohamed Bin Hammam whose position you claim I did not know or appear unfamiliar with. And I have had coffee, talks and both with Mohamed and his team on a daily basis ever since I have arrived in Johannesburg a week ago - you, alas, were nowhere: maybe feverishly reading that other idiot's fiction on the internet instead, were you?

You were never present at single meeting we regularly have as a team and where all positions, not only Mohamed's, have been and are being discussed on a daily basis and based on fact, not infantile hallucinations such as yours. You have no clue about what I said to whom, when and where, yet you proclaim I did not advise the team about this, that or the other: you are completely out of your depth, man. Read a real paper - such as the Sydney Morning Herald of today, and learn. Because if you had a clue, you would have known that this bid, the Australian Bid, is and has always been, perfectly well informed, always ahead of time and development, including the position Mohamed has taken about the 2018 Bid (attached a telling picture, taken yesterday, to express how Mohamed hates us all. Since you live in New York and are clearly unfamiliar with matters Australian, let me enlighten you: he has Australia's Sports Minister, Kate Ellis, by his side to the left and FIFA's legal counsel to his right who sits on a key Committee of the AFC)."

Hargitay attached a photo of Bin Hammam with Ellis and the Australian lawyer and FFA board member Moya Dodd. He continued in emailed rage about Andrew Jennings before hitting the home straight.

"Frankly, dear man, you are so clueless that it is not really worth

ever responding to your maliciously misguided nonsense in any detail. Before you continue with your asinine assumptions, useless fabrications and infantile conclusions about a subject-matter that you have no idea about, take a starters' course in information-gathering and get a life.

Accept that you have no access, no relevance and start building from there. Might prove useful for a future where, after many more years of hard learning, you can start claiming that you are a serious writer. Presently, you cut a sad and lonely figure. You might even find that, sitting in New York City, and writing about matters that you have no clue about, is maybe not the best prerequisite for serious news production.

It is not Australia's bid that is in turmoil. It is your malicious mind.

Peter Hargitay

PS: please do not respond; I won't answer any of your bs ever again. You are a total waste of time.

PPS: By the way: who paid your trip to South Africa?"

Clearly, some kind of nerve had been touched. I emailed FFA and asked if Hargitay was writing to me as an individual or a representative of the sport's governing body in Australia. I also asked if this email was indicative of how the bid should be portrayed. I never heard back. I did respond to Hargitay, however, to tell him the sandwiches I was eating at the Australia-USA game (a friendly before the 2010 World Cup) came from a sandwich shop in a mall I'd picked up on the way to the stadium. I even had the receipt. He couldn't even get his spies to report back correctly.

He would also respond to me again, of course, after I later emailed and asked to clarify his fee after widespread media conjecture couldn't agree on what Australia's taxpayer had paid him for his services. And as for who paid for my trip to South Africa? Hargitay was obsessed with a bizarre theory I had been hired by the US bid for 2026. I had in fact, ridden in on the back of Harry Kewell, a player on the pitch. But that's another story and another better told elsewhere. And as we discovered in December, 2010, history told a story full of facts. Australia's bid for 2022, masterminded by Hargitay, roped in just one single vote and was embarrassingly eliminated in the very first round. The international man of mystery was a mystery no more.

A PHOTO FROM JAMAICA RAISES QUIET QUESTIONS

Kingston, October 2010

Sometimes, the best source for finding out about what was happening with Australia's World Cup bid was not from Football Federation Australia but randomly scanning websites reporting news from Jamaica. Which was exactly how I uncovered an until-then-unannounced (at least by the FFA) deal between Australia and Jamaica that would see a $60 million gift apparently end up in the Caribbean. The day began surfing the internet and by lunch I was trading emails with the office of a government minister in Jamaica.

The result was that Football Federation Australia promised to help Jamaica implement Australian taxpayer-funded projects in the Caribbean to win support for its 2022 World Cup bid. Jamaican government and football officials and senior Australian football official John Boultbee were signatories of the memorandum of understanding between Jamaica and the FFA.

As with many aspects of the Australia bid for the World Cup, it was a strategy that was opaque and confusing. The agreement was trumpeted in the Jamaican press as a means of giving the Caribbean nation's football industry access to $60 million in Australian aid money pledged to the region last year by former prime minister Kevin Rudd. But Australia's Department of Foreign Affairs and Trade said it "has not provided any funding towards this agreement" although it did later launch $60 million commitment to funding programs through the Caribbean Community, a regional organisation that included 15 countries - including Haiti and Suriname - that was unrelated to the World Cup bid.

The FFA pointed out it has pledged to help Jamaica with projects only when aid money is approved for developing football in Jamaica.

"Our objective is to serve up some football-related projects in Jamaica and, eventually, other countries, as possible recipients of funding under the overall government development program," Boultbee, who was the most open person about the deal, said.

The agreement raised eyebrows because it was instigated by Peter Hargitay, a Swiss-Hungarian hired by the FFA as a strategy adviser to influence the FIFA executive committee members, who will vote on the 2022 Cup host in Zurich on December 2.

Mr Hargitay is considered close to controversial FIFA committee member Jack Warner, who is from Trinidad and Tobago and wields huge power in Caribbean football circles. Mr Warner's support for Australia could be crucial in the later stages of the vote.

Boultbee was clear: "The suggestion to consider Jamaica in this context came from Peter Hargitay."

The official handout photograph of the signing ceremony included Jamaica Football Federation president Horace Burrell Olivia Grange, Jamaica's Minister of Youth, Sports and Culture, John Boultbee from FFA, and the usually publicity-shy Hargitay.

Hargitay has strong ties to the island. At the time, his wife was Jamaican and he owned property on the island. In 2006, he received an apology from its government after he was arrested but acquitted of a drug trafficking incident a decade earlier. In 2013, his British-educated daughter Gina was selected as Miss Jamaica World and represented the country at the Miss World Pageant in Bali, Indonesia.

The memorandum of understanding was signed in Kingston, coinciding with a September 27 visit to Jamaica by Warner and FIFA president Sepp Blatter, whom Hargitay had previously advised.

From Kingston, Jamaican sports minister Olivia Grange explained FFA help would be financial or in-kind support such as resources, education and equipment.

"Australian experts and companies will help to implement the various initiatives. Such support will come either from the FFA or Australian agencies directly," she said.

FIFA rules prohibit bidding nations from striking secret deals with officials and member federations to get support for their bids but encourage nations to promote football development in poorer countries.

Australia's courting of the Caribbean has not gone unnoticed in the US, a major rival for the 2022 rights. As chief of the Confederation of North, Central American and Caribbean Association Football (of which Jamaica is a member) Jack Warner will support the US bid during early voting.

"We're very pleased that Australia is spending money in the Caribbean, that's fine, that's a good thing," US Soccer Federation Sunil Gulati said at the Leaders in Football conference in London.

THE BEST MOTORCYCLE MECHANIC IN DILI

Wollongong, September 2009

In his own words, Alfredo Esteves lives a different reality to many of us and that's not just because he's a defender for Wollongong FC in the New South Wales Premier League. In 2008, as well as helping Wollongong win the state championship, the 32-year-old lined up alongside Cristiano Ronaldo, Edgar Davids and Raúl in an All-Stars team selected by Luis Figo for a charity.

That's not the amazing part of the story, however.

Esteves is the captain of Timor-Leste's national team. In 2008, Timor-Leste – previously known as East Timor – climbed from last place in FIFA's official rankings to currently sit 199th out of 208 football-playing nations. History had been made. Timor-Leste had still yet to win a match in its ten-year existence but rocketed up the rankings courtesy of a 2-2 draw against Cambodia in the Asian Football Confederation's regional AFF Cup.

"It was a really big moment for everyone," Esteves said. "Maybe it's difficult to understand but, when you are on the field representing your country, every single improvement makes you feel so good. The first game we ever played against the Philippines, we lost by seven goals. The next one we lost 1-0. Everyone was happy losing just 1-0. When we got the draw against Cambodia it was the cherry on the cake. We didn't think we would get a draw for a long time."

Many people would struggle to find Timor-Leste on a map. That's not unusual. North of Australia and east of Indonesia, the former Portuguese colony was occupied by the Indonesians from 1975 to 1999 and finally gained sovereignty in 2002.

"Timor is a new country and it doesn't have infrastructure for anything," Esteves explained. "But when you travel through the country, soccer is 90 percent of everything. All the kids love to play.

They don't even need a field. They just want to kick the ball around. You see kids everywhere using two rocks to make a goal. They just play for hours.

"There is a lot of talent there and a lot of passion but there are no fields to play the game. There is no regular league. Sometimes, they organise tournaments for clubs to come together but when the tournament is finished there's nothing. Sixty per cent of the population is under 25 but Timor has no jobs. The kids just spend the day hanging out doing nothing."

Esteves is the only professional player in a national team that was eliminated early on the road to the 2010 World Cup in South Africa, courtesy of an 8-1 loss over two games against Hong Kong. National coach Pedro Almeida is a local celebrity but his fame comes not from being a football coach but as one of the best motorcycle mechanics in Timor's capital city, Dili. It is difficult for the coach to select a squad for tournaments. When football doesn't pay, players are too busy providing for their families. Leaving a job for the folly of football, even playing for your country, means there's no one to go fishing, no one to work, no one to bring home a daily meal.

"They can't stop working – they have families to look after," Esteves said. "It's difficult just to focus on soccer. They have to work to support the rest of the family. My teammates all want a chance to play overseas but it's not easy to leave Timor and go somewhere else, even to get a trial. They can't leave their families."

Esteves hopes to finally lead Timor-Leste to a historic first-ever victory. The country faces many challenges, not least from political polarisation that also spills over into national sports administration. Getting things done in such circumstances can be tough but that elusive first win may unite the nation.

"When I played with all those famous players I was representing Timor," Esteves added. "It's something to be proud of, to be Timorese and to be on the same field as those guys. Timor is a small country that has never won anything but we are getting closer. It will be a big celebration, maybe even around the world, when we do win a game.

They have been suffering for many years with all the problems in the country. That first win will be something that will touch the world. It will be a great moment for everyone. It will be progress."

THE SUN SETS INTO THE MEADOWLANDS (AND NO ONE SEES QATAR COMING)

New York, May 2010

China, and not Qatar, was viewed by many as being the spoiler in Australia's bid to host the 2022 World Cup. China's role was, on the surface, passive but was a big part of a geopolitical jigsaw puzzle with each piece weighed down with FIFA politics. If bidding nation A got 2018 then bidding nation B would get 2022 and then what would happen to 2026? Even with its expensive consultants - ones that boasted they were mainlined into FIFA's veins - no one saw Qatar coming.

So here it was that on a Friday May morning in 2010 in Zurich, federal sports minister Kate Ellis, Football Federation Australia chairman Frank Lowy and CEO Ben Buckley officially presented FIFA, soccer's world governing body, with Australia's bid documents to host either the 2018 or 2022 World Cup. It would be a long day. After Australia's allotted 15 minutes, bids from England, Holland and Belgium, Japan, South Korea, Qatar, Russia, Spain and Portugal and the USA enjoyed their own formal ceremonies and answered questions from the media.

The contents of Australia's so-called "Bid Book", the official document, remained secret. We do know it was bound in kangaroo leather, ran to 760 pages, and much of its argument was based on regional proximity to Asia and "world class" stadiums. The problem for Frank Lowy ahead of the December 2 vote that revealed the successful bids? Those very reasons were an argument why the 2022 World Cup would go elsewhere (if we agreed that 2018 would be won by a European bidder).

A week earlier, the new Meadowlands stadium outside of New York opened its doors with a soccer match between Mexico and

Ecuador in front of a 75,000 sell-out crowd. While Australia's bid had wrestled with state governments and the AFL over access to grounds across the country, the new Meadowlands, which replaced the, er, old Meadowlands, was the fourth major state-of-the-art stadium opened in the New York area in the past 12 months.

"These type of buildings are built regularly in the United States and these buildings have to be built with an international football crowd in mind," explained David Downs, the executive director of the US bid, in one of the stadium's luxury hospitality suites before the opening game. Importantly, no public funds are required for the US bid campaign, nor to build infrastructure, should it win. That's unlike Australia, which has received $46 million from the federal government to fund its bid, with more to be spent on stadium upgrades. Domestically, the AFL and NRL are nervous about the prospect of a World Cup in Australia, blocking access to stadiums or demanding compensation. Things are different in America.

"I can tell you they are all encouraging our bid," Downs said of other sports in the US. "We met with the NBA about approaching several NBA players to endorse our bid. They were delighted that we were going to reach out to them."

The American venues made a compelling case for 2022 but Asia, considered the future of football, made compelling economic sense. Australia's Asian approach was right to a point but, the reality is that, for FIFA, Asia really means "China".

"There is no way the 2022 World Cup will go to Asia, because that would shut China out for up to 20 years," said one football official with a direct line to FIFA's executive committee. "If FIFA is serious about opening up Asia then the launch pad for that is really China, not Japan, Korea, Qatar, or even Australia."

Still, in August 2010, FFA CEO Ben Buckley left Australia for a secret mission to China. We know this trip was secret because FFA refused to tell anyone anything about it.

"It is not our policy to publicly discuss this sort of information as I am sure you understand," emailed Rod Allen, FFA's head of Media

Relations, when he was quizzed about the nature of Buckley's trip.

Understand? Well, since you ask, not really.

Buckley's no-need-to-know jaunt included a stopover in Osaka, Japan, on the return leg and was, of course, tied to Australia's taxpayer-funded bid to the 2022 FIFA World Cup. There was some surprise from within the wider Australian sports community - and those with knowledge of how World Cup bids are won - of the need to visit China but the truth is that at that time, four months until the vote, FFA needed all the friends it could muster in Asia.

AFC president Mohammed Bin Hammam had recently declared he'd vote for his home country Qatar to host 2022 rather than any of the other AFC bidders – Australia, Japan, and South Korea. Peter Hargitay, one of the Australian bid's controversial consultants, visited China at least twice in 2009 on FFA business. The outcome from those trips was a belief that China could come out on Australia's side for the 2022 bid.

Subsequent plans included a final presentation to FIFA in Zurich in December featuring Mandarin-speaking Prime Minister Kevin Rudd as well as a delegation from China backing Australia's World Cup proposal as a tournament for all of Asia. FFA was confident it had an endorsement from the China Football Association, which was timetabled to be publicly revealed around August. But, as Rudd might have known, 12 months is as long a time in football as it is in politics.

The then-head of the China Football Association, Nan Yong, who supposedly gave Australia his blessing ended up in jail facing trial for alleged corruption related to bribes, match-fixing, and betting. Go figure. The new boss of Chinese football, Wei Di, was apparently an incorruptible with a mandate from the government to aggressively clean up China's image in international football. And guess who suddenly wanted to host the 2026 World Cup? China.

"There have been many debates on whether China should host a World Cup or when to host it," Wei Dei said after the 2010 World Cup. "After the tournament succeeded in South Africa, I have to admit, China has no reason not to have a World Cup. And now is the time."

That announcement didn't go down too well in Australia or Qatar, or Japan or South Korea. FIFA won't hold successive tournaments in the same region and China is the mother lode when it comes to soccer taking over the global sports market. The winning formula would now expect to look like Europe in 2018, USA four years later, and China in 2026.

Wei Di's enthusiasm for a China World Cup did not go unnoticed across Asia and he was soon sought to clarify exactly what he meant. The Australian government went so far as to ask the Chinese Football Association boss exactly what he was lobbying for and whether China was supporting an Asian bid for 2022.

"I never said that I did not want to see any of the Asian countries host the 2022 World Cup," Wei, said. "The report comes from nowhere. Such reports damage China's image. Officials from the Australian embassy even called us and wanted us to explain. I know four Asian countries are bidding for the 2022 World Cup. But it does not mean China cannot bid for 2026. We can still bid for it, even if an Asian country hosts the 2022 event."

Buckley's week away came at a time when FFA is putting out a series of domestic fires.

FFA stayed well away from an avoidable public feud between Harry Kewell and Robbie Slater, two of the sports biggest names in Australia, but the organization did step in aggressively to ban two A-League players accused of "diving".

This was an honorable and brave attempt to stamp out perceived cheating but was mismanaged when the accused players were unable to mount appeals for what is widely agreed were highly debatable incidents – even under video scrutiny. While the World Cup bid was in full swing Buckley, a keen micro-manager, oversaw the A-League, soccer's local barometer, under pressure. Crowds were low and, in some cases, lower than the old National Soccer League.

Expansion teams Gold Coast United and North Queensland Fury were near disaster and few people seem to have any interest in Melbourne Heart, the second team for Melbourne. Newcastle Jets recently joined Adelaide United and North Queensland on a list of teams propped up financially by the governing body. Sydney Rovers, a proposed second team for Sydney, was going to enter the league in 2011 after being granted a licence with no financial backers and amid cries about lack of transparency for the A-League admission process.

Buckley's contract expired at the end of 2010, just after the December 2 announcement on where the 2016 and 2022 World cups will be held. If there was a vote on his tenure, it's unlikely Australia's football community would tick a box with any confidence - even if Buckley had returned from Beijing with news China had dropped its 2026 ambition to support Australia's bid for 2022. But then the public wouldn't know about that because – ssshhh – this sort of thing isn't discussed publicly.

Understand?

It turned out only a few people really did understand. And those people were very quiet on Qatar's chances.

BEWARE OF FRIENDS WITH PRIVATE JETS

Johannesburg, June 2010

For the Australians in South Africa, Wednesday morning began with the best intentions.

Federal Sports Minister Kate Ellis accompanied Football Federation Australia Chairman Frank Lowy and his CEO Ben Buckley to Mohklakano, a township west of Johannesburg. The town's welcome included a vuvuzela parade through its streets while a bus shuttling Australian media (aka what was supposed to be the World Cup bid cheer squad) was mobbed as if Bafana Bafana, South Africa's soccer team, were inside.

The Australians were in town to donate 9000 'lap desks' to local school kids, a worthy cause costing FFA around $150,000. A fair price for goodwill and great publicity. But whirring away in the minds of both Lowy and Buckley were comments made the day before at a meeting of the Asian Football Confederation. AFC President Mohamed Bin Hammam had announced that his Confederation, of which Australia is a member, will be backing a European nation to host the 2018 World Cup. But, wait - isn't Australia bidding for the 2018 tournament? Ah, yes, and there was Lowy and Buckley's problem.

Quizzed by Australian media as hundreds of Mohlakano primary school students sang, danced, and clapped hands behind them, Lowy and Buckley tried to find positive spin - any spin - about Bin Hammam's comments.

"Who said he is not supporting Australia?" Lowy said. "Okay, so he is not supporting 2018, but [he's] supporting us for 2022."

Buckley, however, revealed that Australia had no idea that Bin Hammam was going to announce Asia's support for a European 2018 candidate: "It was not a position that had been put forward to us prior to the meeting but it doesn't change anything."

Actually, it does. Australia's relationship with AFC has been revealed as something similar to an open marriage. You do your thing. We'll do ours. Don't tell the children. Still, one question Lowy will want answered is why one of his infamous international consultants did not know about the AFC's intention - or at least tell him about Bin Hammam's plan.

Swiss-Hungarian Peter Hargitay is a former adviser to FIFA President Sepp Blatter and previously worked with Bin Hammam before signing on with Australia for this World Cup bid. But despite Hargitay's long list of contacts - and expensive invoices - he appears to have been unable to forewarn FFA of Bin Hammam's plans.

The other question: why didn't Bin Hammam advise Lowy personally of his public announcement? Australia joined AFC in 2005 and, at the time, much was made of the personal relationship forged between the two as they rode around Asia on Lowy's private jet. It was believed that their growing friendship played a large role in Bin Hammam supporting Australia in its bid to join Asia. But maybe not any more.

Buckley believes Australia's relationship with AFC members remains strong, but behind the scenes there appears to be much tension, as demonstrated by Bin Hammam's unguarded moment. South Korea, Japan and Qatar are all bidding for 2022, along with Australia and the United States.

"While there is an enormous amount of respect for one another and the strengths of each bid you can't have a unified position going into the bid because each country is going for its own advantage," Buckley said.

"The relationship [within Asia] is very positive. We are only relative newcomers to the AFC. Everywhere we go in Asia we get a good reception. We have very good representation on a number of important committees. I think Australia is a respected member of the AFC."

That's a great take but another reason Australia's relationship with AFC may be tested is not just because Bin Hammam is Qatari and has to be seen backing his home country, even if he is a pan-continental president. The guy has sights on Sepp Blatter's job, which will be decided in elections next year after the World Cup hosts for 2018 and 2022 are decided.

For Australia, this may be inconsequential but will have big consequences on its 2018/2022 ambition. While the bid bandwagon rolled into Mohklakano, News Limited papers reported Australia "is firming as the likely winner of the 2022 World Cup bid", with Lowy quoted as saying: "I am talking to the people who matter and I hear what they say. I hear their sentiments and I am hearing some very good sentiments about Australia."

As we would later learn, sentiment is one thing. Votes are another thing entirely.

THE FOOTBALLERS WOULD HEAD IN ONE DIRECTION AND THE SOLDIERS TAKE ANOTHER TO WAR

Saigon, 2017

There will be no ceremonies, no medals, and no marches to commemorate this week's 50th anniversary of one of Australia's less-celebrated engagements with Asia. There might be a few phone calls among the former Socceroos who played in Saigon during the height of the Vietnam War to reminisce about dodging landmines during a training session but - other than that - nothing.

Australia was one of eight teams that took part in the 1967 National Day tournament, an event in November that year that included national football teams of South Vietnam, South Korea, New Zealand, Malaysia, Hong Kong, Singapore, and Thailand. The tournament, involving teams from countries supporting the South during the war, was cooked up by South Vietnamese football authorities, effectively an extension of the government.

The Australian army had already realised soccer was a powerful tool in engaging with the Vietnamese and a visit to Australia by South Vietnam Prime Minister Air Vice-Marshal Nguyen Cao Ky in early 1967 sealed Australia's participation in the event.

On the pitch, the tournament - known in Vietnamese as the Quoc Khanh Cup - was a major success for Australia. Coached by "Uncle" Joe Vlasits, a Hungarian who emigrated to Australia in 1949, the Australians was undefeated and beat South Korea in the final in front of a full stadium to win its first trophy in Asia. However, mystery still surrounds who was responsible for agreeing to send the Australians to a war zone in the first place.

Australia had failed to qualify for the 1966 World Cup in England after losing in a play-off against North Korea in Cambodia in 1965. The Australian Soccer Federation was keen for the next generation

- captained by the late Johnny Warren - to gain more experience in Asia ahead of qualifiers for the 1970 World Cup. Saigon was perfect but the Australian government's official role in the wartime exercise is unclear.

"The matter was discussed up to Cabinet level but the file on the deliberations was never transferred to the National Archives and is now lost," Deakin University historian Roy Hay, whose book *Football and War: Australia and Vietnam 1967–1972*, details the tournament.

"I had the late Malcolm Fraser, who was Minister for the Army at the time, on his hands and knees trying to find if there was anything in his files relating to the matter. Fraser was dead against civilian activities in Vietnam and wanted everything done by military people in the chain of command."

Saigon in 1967 was not the city it is today. The Presidential Palace was shelled as the Australian team arrived and it was later revealed Vietcong fighters were arrested for apparently attempting to blow up the South Korean team staying at the same hotel as the Australians. Johnny Warren would often speak about the Vietnam trip - publicly and privately - before his 2004 death and described players being warned about retrieving stray balls during training sessions - the adjoining fields were full of landmines.

Blasts and mortars could be heard during the night as the players tried to sleep. Mine detectors lined the pitch of the Cong Hoa Stadium - today known as Thong Nha Stadium - where the tournament was held. During games, spectators were wary of young children approaching the stands in case they were carrying bombs. Two years prior, an attack at the stadium killed 11 Vietnamese - including four children - and injured 42.

"It looked insane when we were coming in to land when we arrived and you would see military aircraft and bomb craters," said Ron Corry, one of the Australian team's goalkeepers. "We were told that it was safe and that the war hadn't really hit Saigon but it wasn't very far away. At night we used to be able to sit up on the roof and watch the tracer bullet flares go up and fly across the sky and you would hear the big guns."

Corry, now 76, recalled that a friend from Australia met the team at the airport and helped arrange access to Australian military facilities in Saigon.

"My mate had been conscripted and was stationed at Saigon," said Corry. "He organised for us to get into the army mess and have a decent meal and a beer and watch a movie. The Australian soldiers would tell us if we heard one shot, don't worry about it. If we heard two shots, get a little worried. If we heard three, hit the floor. The Vietcong would try to come in on bikes and leave bombs."

The Australians were warned by team doctor Brian Corrigan, the Australian Olympic team's top medic from 1968 to 1988, to not drink Saigon's water and instead drink beer to hydrate.

"We didn't need much convincing to drink the beer," joked Corry.

A Qantas representative travelling with the team also secured access to American military facilities where the team ate with American soldiers. They would often have incongruous partings from the mess halls - the footballers would head in one direction to play soccer and the Australian and American soldiers take another to war.

During the tournament the team flew to Vung Tau, an Australian logistics base south of Saigon, to meet Australian troops and play a match against them. The team flew in an RAAF Caribou and, according to a *Sydney Morning Herald* report at the time, players were told to ignore the bullet holes in the aircraft.

"The Caribous had open doors at the back and we flew across the sea about 10 feet above the water," said Corry.

Johnny Warren wrote in his autobiography, *Sheilas, Wogs, and Poofters*, that the trip occasionally resembled something out of a Hollywood war movie. "*Good Morning Vietnam* reminds me of the scenes we were thrown into," he recalled.

Far from the five-star luxury now afforded Australia's sporting teams, the Australians were billeted four to a room sharing bunk beds. Two players were electrocuted by the hotel's rudimentary wiring.

"We built great camaraderie on that tour," said Ron Corry, who later coached National Soccer League club Wollongong Wolves and was an assistant coach with A-League side Western Sydney Wanderers.

"That is lost with a lot of the Aussie teams. Everyone is more of a mercenary now. If they get beaten playing for Australia, they're on the plane the next day home going off to get $10,000 a week [with their clubs]. The players in our squad played with a passion for their country that you don't see now. Today, some of them don't play with passion - they are just playing another game."

According to Roy Hay, the Vietnam Football Federation paid the Australian team's airfares and accommodation during the tour. The Australian Soccer Federation requested a $10,000 subsidy from Australia's Department of External Affairs to cover some costs but it's not known if that money was ever received. The players, most of whom had jobs at home, received $50 a week wages plus a weekly allowance of $10 during the trip. They were told they could keep their team tracksuits as a reward for winning the tournament.

Warren long maintained the trip's purpose was for propaganda amid growing opposition at home to Australia's involvement in the war. Roy Hay recalls Noel St Clair Deschamps, Australian Ambassador to Cambodia in 1965 when Australia played North Korea in the World Cup play-off, claiming the Australian team's presence in Cambodia was "worth at least £100 million in foreign aid" and recommended the team tour south-east Asia annually.

"He had never been aware Australia had possessed such a powerful propaganda and goodwill weapon as its soccer team," said Hay.

While entertainers received public recognition as well as the Vietnam Logistic and Support Medal for performing in Vietnam, the Australian football team received nothing. In 2005, the government claimed only individuals who were under government or military jurisdiction during their time in Vietnam were eligible for official recognition. The tracksuits were all the soccer team would receive.

"I think we were probably in more danger than any of them," said Corry of the recognition celebrities and musicians received for visiting troops in Vietnam. "We were right in it while the entertainers would be out at the army bases which were pretty well protected. Someone has said that we should get a medal but I don't know. It could have been dangerous but we considered it more of an adventure."

Within a few months of the tournament, much had changed. Australian Prime Minister Harold Holt was dead, the Tet offensive was underway, and anti-war activism was on the rise. For the players, though, the Vietnam National Day tournament would live on. Every year, until his death, Johnny Warren would receive a Christmas Card from teammate Atti Abonyi: "Remember the tunnel in Vietnam". The quip referred to the Australian team's entrance to the playing field in front of a huge crowd before the 1967 final against South Korea.

"I still remember the hairs standing up on the back of my neck," Warren recalled.

THERAPY

Istanbul, February 2009 - New York, November 2018

"Everything that you need is here," said Harry Kewell as we stood by the open window of his apartment in Istanbul. "Istanbul is an eye opener. The people are fantastic. The club is fantastic. The food is great. Driving a car is a little bit crazy but I quite enjoy a challenge."

It was late in the afternoon and the sun was about to set. Kewell stopped talking and held up his hand as if to say "listen". In the distance was an evening call to prayer. The singing came from the top of a nearby minaret atop mosque. Within a minute, one and two and three and four and five more calls could be heard from nearby mosques filling the city with songs.

"It's amazing," Kewell said. "I could listen to it all night. It's definitely a different culture for me here and there are things that I would normally not see."

Kewell raised eyebrows with his move to Galatasaray in 2008, even if the Turkish champions were a massive club with huge support and regularly competed in European competition. A free agent after Liverpool decided against renewing his contract, Kewell had options across Europe, perhaps a surprise considering his injury record. Italian club Juventus began a flirtation earlier that year that came close to consummation. Premier League sides Portsmouth, Aston Villa, Fulham, and Tottenham joined Roma, Milan, and Valencia as suitors.

Many of those clubs tied contracts to appearance-related payments or, most importantly for the player, nixed the idea of Australian physiotherapist Les Gelis having a role with the player's fitness programs. Gelis was acknowledged in Kewell circles as a miracle worker and was pretty much employed full-time overseeing everything from daily Pilates sessions to warming up the million dollar limbs before a game. Galatasaray just wanted to know what time Kewell could start.

"From day one, Galatasaray obliged and were up front," Kewell said. "I had other clubs saying that if I broke down injured then this would happen or that would happen, which was all bullshit. Then a club like Galatasaray says yes, let's go."

There was another piece to the jigsaw put together to rebuild Kewell's stalled career. Good form with Galatasaray would rehabilitate Kewell's reputation as one of the most exciting players of his generation. Prior to signing with the Turkish club, Kewell was handed a list of players – including French World Cup stars Franck Ribery and Nicolas Anelka – who had played in Turkey and reinvented themselves.

"If this was a book, then the last five years would be sealed together," Kewell added as the call to prayer wound down. He was referring to his time at Liverpool where he had suffered with astonishing injuries that should have ended his career – and would have ended the careers of many other players who experienced the same setbacks. "It is almost like the story would jump straight from when I was at Leeds to Galatasaray."

Which is one reason he is telling me all this. As things would play out, all this was indeed planned to be a book, maybe even two. Eighteen months after that conversation in Turkey I signed a contract with a publisher to write Kewell's official biography - as well as a proposed diary during the 2010 World Cup in South Africa. The plan was to deliver a story that would be quite unlike any other account of life as a professional footballer – especially an Australian one. But, as with many things to do with Harry Kewell, things would get complicated and the greatest and most well-intentioned plans would never quite be realized. Harry Kewell would remain the greatest story never told.

"You're like my therapist," Kewell laughed one afternoon. We'd talk at least once a week, either on the phone, or on Skype, or in person if we were in the same location. When the biography project started, he was living by himself in Istanbul, sometimes with his physiotherapist as a roommate. His wife and family were in Manchester. For Kewell, his time in Istanbul was football and football and football. He'd tell me how he felt sorry for his 24/7 physiotherapist because of the hard time he would give him. We took deep dives into his playing career and life off the pitch, trying to wipe away the professional veneer that made football, well, a profession.

I first met Kewell face-to-face in 1998, just prior to the World Cup that Kewell should have been playing at with Australia. Instead, we stood in a park in Smithfield, western Sydney, a few blocks from his childhood home, where he grew up the youngest of three children to Helen and Rod. "Me and my brother [Rod junior] did everything," recalls Kewell, who also has an old sister, Jacqueline. "Golf, tennis, cricket, swimming, basketball, rugby union. There were about 10 of us on the street always playing something." Kewell prefers not to speak publicly about his family. "They are just normal people living normal lives," he says.

We were there for a photo shoot for the magazine *Inside Sport* who previously had little interest in Australian soccer, the editor believing there were few stories to tell about it. A young Kewell who was at Leeds United was a story, apparently. The photographer had Kewell pose by some park goalposts and asked him to take his shirt off for a picture. Kewell responded with a grimace and one word: "Seriously?"

Harry Kewell developed a taste for football at age four, showed serious early promise and attended Westfields Sports High – a Sydney school that specialises in sports – before accepting an offer to join Leeds United in England. A scholarship from a charity, the Big Brother Movement, allowed Kewell and another aspiring footballer called Brett Emerton to visit Leeds United for an extended trial. Kewell and Emerton travelled to England together and landed at Heathrow airport. There was no one to meet them and they had no real idea of where they were going.

Legend has it they figured out the London Underground, and worked out they had to head north by train from London to Leeds. They arrived at Elland Road, Leeds United's stadium, and knocked on a door and announced they had a arrived for a trial. They were told they were at the wrong place and needed to be at Thorp Arch, the club's training ground an hour north of the city by public transport. Still, when they got onto the Leeds training pitch, both young players impressed. Leeds wanted both to stay. Kewell, with help from his father's British ancestry, got a break. Emerton returned to Sydney.

Aged 17, in 1996, Kewell made his debut for Australia against Chile in Antofagasta. "When we arrived in Chile, Harry was very quiet and wouldn't say boo to a mouse," recalls Andy Bernal, who played his final match for Australia on the night Kewell played his first. "But as soon as he got the ball on the training field, it was the older guys who were the ones who couldn't say anything. You know straight away when someone is special."

Before the match, the Chilean hosts hosed down Australia's dressing room and turned out the lights to test their mettle. The game was supposed to be a friendly. "We were a bit pissed off but for a young kid like Harry he wasn't bothered," recalls Bernal. "To him, it was all fun and games."

If the Chile match was a whisper to the Australian public, in November 1997 Kewell's presence with the national team was a loud shout. The Socceroos played the first-leg of the World Cup play-off with Iran in Tehran. To outsiders, Kewell came from nowhere to be selected. But within 20 minutes, the mystery man was on his way to stardom.

"I was surprised by his self-confidence," Robbie Slater told me before he had an infamous falling out with Kewell after the 2010 World Cup "He was just a kid and we were playing in front of 128,000 Iranian fans, all men. They wouldn't let women watch. We couldn't hear each other on the pitch but after about 15 minutes Harry seemed at home."

Kewell got drawn into a fracas with an Iranian player in the opening minutes of the game but was reined in by older teammate Aurelio Vidmar. Displaying his ability to rise to the challenge at hand, he soon answered with an exquisite goal. "The Iranian fans were spitting and throwing things," says Slater, "but after that goal I have never heard a louder silence." A week later, Kewell scored again, this time Australia's first goal in front of a packed Melbourne Cricket Ground. With floppy teenage hair, he celebrated by miming into a corner flag as if it was a microphone. Ladies and gentlemen, introducing Harry Kewell.

Ten years later Kewell was a multi-millionaire earning $250,000 a week, solely from his basic club contact with Liverpool. Add to that bonuses for winning matches and scoring goals, as well as lucrative endorsement contracts with Adidas, the Nine Network, BT Financial, Sony, and Pepsi and it was easy to see why Kewell was in another stratosphere compared to almost every other Australian sportsperson. He lived in Hale, on the outskirts of Manchester, close to a major airport and 90 minutes on the motorway from Liverpool's training ground. When he drove to his job he could choose between a black Ford Mustang, a black Hummer, and black Mercedes CSL 55 AMG. If he tires of black, he can take his grey Porsche GT3 for a spin.

But - it's a cliché because it is true - money didn't buy happiness. If Harry Kewell wanted to glue together the pages that would describe his time at Liverpool, it was not without reason. The frustration from injuries, that culminated in the 2005 UEFA Champions League final where he limped off after 20 minutes, cut deep. Not just for the player but for the fans and hyper-critical media.

"Ya see over there?" said one skinny Liverpool fan, dressed in a tracksuit with close-cropped hair. He'd appointed himself my personal guide around Anfield one morning when I was visiting the club and pointed to a gate between two derelict terraced houses one block from the stadium. "That's where Harry Kewell used to park his car during matches. After games, we would gather around, bang on the roof, and tell him he was fuckin' useless."

The British media could be even more abrasive. Harry had no heart, wrote Richard Williams in The *Guardian*, dismissing his ill-fated appearance in the Champions League final where he limped off with a torn adductor muscle as "a player with a heart the size of a diamond ear-stud". Other commentators accused him of earning big money, playing in cruise control, picking up his cheque and going home.

"You read things in the paper and it's horrible," Kewell said. "I know it's not true, my family know it is not true, my close friends know it's not true, all the Liverpool staff and players know it's not true but anyone outside thinks it is true. I just wish people would get the truth. Then I think a player would mend quicker, mentally and physically."

Which is a neat way to drag us to South Africa and the 2010 World Cup. The idea had been to speak with Kewell every day and document his World Cup campaign. The 2006 World Cup had been filled with high and low and high drama evidenced by Kewell's goal against Croatia and subsequent appearance at the Italy game on crutches. There was every reason to think 2010 could have similar drama - which would prove true but not in the way most people would have imagined.

Documenting Kewell was not going to be easy, however. For months, executives at Football Federation Australia had tried to get my media accreditation for the tournament denied after I'd been critical of its failing World Cup bid. One executive pointed out that banning a journalist for not toeing the company line was not a great media strategy and eventually the organisation approved the accreditation.

The Australian team spent almost two weeks in Johannesburg before the tournament and each night, after the team dinner, Kewell would call or text with an invitation to meet. The catch was that media was not allowed in the team hotel so we were presented with a scene that should have been in a comedy movie. I would be snuck in through the back door of one of Johannesburg's fanciest hotels and be whisked up an elevator to meet Kewell. We would hang out in a room and I would, indeed, be his therapist. The even funnier part was that his teammates knew about our meetings, as did senior coaching staff (head coach Pim Verbeek requested discretion and to obviously not disrupt the team). The challenge was bypassing FFA officials - many distracted anyway by campaigning for the 2018 and 2022 World Cup bids.

As with the 2006 World Cup, Kewell faced a fitness battle to be ready for the first game - this time against Germany in Durban. He'd had surgery on his groin earlier in the year, had barely played an hour of football before the tournament, but worked overtime to be fit for the World Cup. Come game day against Germany, however, he was ready to start. Verbeek decided Kewell would serve the team better on the bench but Australia was embarrassingly beaten 4-0 by the Germans. Verbeek was panned for his tactics and Tim Cahill was needlessly sent off to add to the chaos.

And then everything went nuts.

Mike Cockerill was one of the most passionate fans of Australian football you could ever meet. It also turned out his day job was writing about Australian football for the *Sydney Morning Herald*. He'd been an evangelist for the local game and lived the highs and many, many, lows. In 1996, when I started showing up at National Soccer League games and Soccer Australia press conferences he'd asked "who's taking your copy?" He found it difficult to believe anyone who didn't have to fill 250 words for a city newspaper would be as intrigued as him by the drama and nuances of the local game but here I was working angles for magazines in Australia and Europe.

We crossed paths at the 1998 World Cup in France and went drinking in 2002 in various bars in Kyoto and Kobe and Tokyo where we were the only Australian writers reporting on the world's biggest sporting event - in our time zone and in our region. Cockerill was representing Fairfax Media - which published the *Sydney Morning Herald* and *The Age*. I was a freelancer winging it on a freelance budget, writing for the Sunday Fairfax papers, calling in tournament updates to disinterested talk show radio hosts, and writing a diary for a British magazine. In 2006, when Australia finally did qualify for the World Cup, we were both part of a bloated Fairfax team riddled with egos and hierarchies that I wanted no part of. Neither did Cockerill.

This was when I learned engaging a cranky Cockerill was akin to facing a force 10 hurricane and an experience to avoid at all costs. Fairfax has messed up its accommodation plans for its now-abundant bandwagon of journalists covering Australia's campaign in Germany. Writers and photographers had been billeted in what was effectively a trucker's motel outside of Stuttgart, 90 minutes from the Australian team's training base and where all the action was in nearby Oehringen.

We would face three hours on the road every day just to get to and from training and risk missing any team scoops to rivals. The photographers, who could never miss a photo opportunity, threatened mutiny. Cockerill and I debated our strategy on how to fix this screw up as he drove us from the truck stop motel to Oehringen on the German autobahn at 180 kilometres per hour, white-knuckle testing if it was at all possible to cut the travel time to an hour. I told him I was going to abandon the motel and move to town with the photographers - as a freelancer I would get a new hotel paid for somehow. Cockerill was also a faithful company man who believed everyone should stick together: "I haven't finally got to a fucking World Cup with Australia to cover it from a shitty hotel where no one knows it is on," After much on the ground discussion and many phone calls around the world, Fairfax wouldn't relent and the writers stayed with the truckers (one, subsequently, rarely leaving his hotel room). The photographers moved north. I went with them.

In 2010, Cockerill was still motivated by making sure Australia was taken seriously on the world stage. The loss to Germany in Durban, however, hurt. Cockerill railed against the "Dutch coaching mafia" but in a post-match column turned a flamethrower on Harry Kewell - who hadn't even played in the game. It was an astonishing blaze of vindictive writing that torched Kewell, attacking his celebrity and his record with injuries.

He lambasted Kewell for not warming up with other substitutes - even though Australia's coaching staff had told him not to. He criticised Kewell for hugging one of Germany's coaches and for talking to his family in the crowd after the game. It was an extraordinary column, ballsy as anything, except Mike's ferocious ire was off the rails and inexplicably misdirected. I knew this having sat through, day after day, Kewell's effort to be ready for the Germany game.

The afternoon after the column appeared online, Kewell fronted the post-training mixed zone to put in his own fiery performance. He called for Cockerill to "show himself" only to discover the writer was missing the Australian training session in favour of travelling to see South Africa play Uruguay in Pretoria. Cockerill's absence was normal but not great optics that further fueled a conspiracy theory. Kewell unrolled a blistering volley on Cockerill and the media.

"It's a shame," Kewell said. "Youse are all supposed to be on our team and it's a shame that youse are all having a go at us."

That was a common refrain among many footballers - that the media was supposed to cheerlead the team and not apply critical thinking to its dynamics and performances. Ironically, the Australian team's top media officer at the 2010 World Cup, unabashed rugby league fan Rod Allen, had been Fairfax Media's sports editor - the boss of the coverage - during the 2006 World Cup. It wasn't as if there was no one within the organisation to advise Kewell on how to respond to Cockerill's column in public.

"I think there are people that are just making things up," Kewell said.

This was the moment the 2006 honeymoon was over for Australian football. The party was officially done. The Golden Generation was no more (proven by its Asian Cup fiasco in 2007) and Australian football was eating itself alive. A giant like Cockerill, who had seen it all, unleashed years of frustration on Kewell, a rare player he had never built a relationship with. Kewell, in turn, threw back years of frustration at the media inaccurately reporting on his motivation ("He wanted to play for England not Australia", some falsely claimed) and his "weak" state of mind (his mind and commitment were incredibly strong). Wearing my therapist hat, as the love affair ended in tears, I would have recommended marriage counselling for everyone.

"Actually DO something," Cockerill asked Kewell in a follow up column. "Prove something."

At least we were talking about our feelings, even if they were not the actual reality. For the opening 24 minutes in the next game against Ghana, Kewell did do something. Kewell, inserted into the starting lineup, was everywhere and was keen to prove something. Australia took an early 1-0 lead. Kewell was all over the pitch and seemed to want to demonstrate how hard he could work for the team - maybe too hard. At one point he found himself on the goal line, defending a shot. It was a goal-bound rocket that that struck his arm. It was impossible to avoid but a penalty to Ghana. Red card to Kewell. Harsh. But his World Cup was over. It summed up 2010.

The planned World Cup diary was now too short to publish (and a little dull) and as events that rolled out over the next few years would reveal, the greatest story never told remains that way. Kewell eventually left Istanbul and its calls to prayer and pitched up in Melbourne for a season with Melbourne Victory. He added his name to the list of Australian players with excellent careers in Europe that underwhelmed when they played in the A-League.

Kewell also parted ways with his manager Bernie Mandic in 2011, a relationship that lasted 14 years and ran parallel to Kewell at the peak of his powers. While Kewell focused on the pitch and his fitness, Mandic ran Kewell Inc with his brother Nik and turned the kid from Smithfield into one of Australian sport's most successful businesses. A legal settlement between Kewell and Mandic - it took years to untangle the relationship - meant neither could discuss the other in public. A biography where Mandic was a gatekeeper to much of the story's highs and lows became very complicated. Kewell went to ground, resurfacing in time for the book contract to be torn up. Like much to do with Harry Kewell, there's a lot that is unresolved and unfulfilled, a lot of it complicated by third parties and lawyers and half-truths and not quite all the story.

Still, like all good therapists, the secrets are safe with me.

Want some more really good football books from Fair Play Publishing?

Encyclopedia of Socceroos - Every National Team Player
by Andrew Howe

The World Cup Chronicles - 31 Days that Rocked Brazil
by Jorge Knijnik

Playing for Australia The First Socceroos, Asia and World Football
by Trevor Thompson

Support Your Local League - A South East Asian Football Odessy
by Antony Sutton

Introducing Jarrod Black
Part 1 of the Jarrod Black series by Texi Smith

Jarrod Black - Hospital Pass
Part 2 of the Jarrod Black series by Texi Smith

Coming Soon:

Soccer in Australia to 1949
by Peter Kunz

Encyclopedia of Matildas - Every National Team Player
by Andrew Howe and Greg Werner

From US partners, Powderhouse Press:

Whatever It Takes - the Inside Story of the FIFA Way
by Bonita Mersiades

Find them all at www.fairplaypublishing.com.au

www.ingramcontent.com/pod-product-compliance
Lightning Source LLC
Chambersburg PA
CBHW052307300426
44110CB00035B/2066